SANTERÍA

SANTERÍA

AFRICAN SPIRITS IN AMERICA

JOSEPH M. MURPHY

WITH A NEW PREFACE

BEACON PRESS

BOSTON

Beacon Press
25 Beacon Street
Boston, Massachusetts 02108

Beacon Press books
are published under the auspices of
the Unitarian Universalist Association of Congregations.

04 03 02 01 00   7 8 9 10 11

Text design by Judi Rettich

Library of Congress Cataloging-in-Publication Data

Murphy, Joseph M., 1951–
Santeria : African spirits in America:
with a new preface / Joseph M. Murphy.
    p.   cm.
Includes bibliographical references and index.
ISBN 0-8070-1021-9 (pbk.)
1. Santeria (Cult)   I. Title.
BL2532.S3M86 1993
299'.67—dc20   92–8590

CONTENTS

PREFACE TO THE 1992 EDITION

Since the publication of this book in 1988, I have had the opportunity to speak with priests and priestesses of *santería* from all over the United States. Perhaps the most impressive thing that has been brought home to me is the increasingly public nature of the religion as more and more people come forward to identify themselves with it. For most of the history of santeria in its diaspora, leaders have been concerned with defining the tradition solely for themselves and their own initiates. In the United States during the past ten years, however, a number of leaders have felt called upon to develop institutions and texts to present the religion to a variety of outsiders, ranging from municipal authorities to news media to spiritual seekers. While the community that welcomed me in the Bronx in the late 1970s and early 1980s was devoted to protecting its privacy, other individuals and communities have since taken on public roles as clearinghouses for information about the religion and as organizers of cultural activities for the wider community.

This institutionalization of the religion may have something to do with the nature of the immigrant experience in the United States. The leadership of the community described in this book was composed of immigrants from Cuba, who, for a variety of thoughtful reasons, were reluctant to draw attention to their practice of a non–Judeo-Christian religion in this country. Younger leaders, many of them American born, have been more outspoken in asserting their rights to the free exercise of religion in America and they have had to defend them against considerable opposition from municipal and ecclesiastic authorities. The most notable example of the perils of the public practice of the religion is the case of Hialeah, Florida's Church of Lukumi Babaluaye. Incorporated as a church, this community lost an extended challenge in the courts, where they sought the right to slaughter animals in the prayerful manner prescribed by tradition.[1]

The news media's coverage of *santería* has focused its attention exclusively on the slaughter of animals or the practice of the religion by drug dealers. It has never been their interest to examine the religion's import for the hundreds of thousands of Americans for whom it is a part of daily life. When grisly evidence of the ritual murder of human beings was unearthed in Matamoros, Mexico, in the spring of 1989, reporters and law enforcement authorities were slow to accept that such murders were not "extensions" of the ritual slaughter of animals for food. It came to light that the killers in Matamoros were not inspired by their associations with an African religion, but with a Hollywood image of one. They testified that they repeatedly watched a tape of the feature film *The Believers*, which characterizes African religions as cults of human sacrifice.

These sensationalized news stories have fueled debates in municipalities in Florida and California concerning legislation aimed specifically at practitioners of santeria and other traditions that slaugher animals under ritual conditions. In the face of these new challenges, priests and priestesses have felt it necessary to provide a measure of reliable information to authorities and media and to bring the religion into the light of public scrutiny.

Yet this new public posture presents a number of difficulties for the tradition. Beyond the reprisals of religious intolerance, one of the problems in bringing the religion before the public is the commitment of the tradition to oral teaching. Knowledge in the religion is based on initiation. Only those who carry certain initiations are sanctioned to attend certain ceremonies, learn certain ritual information, or know the increasingly esoteric meanings of rhythms, songs, greetings, gestures, foods, and herbs. This emphasis on secrecy has the positive value of preserving the personal transmission of teachings, but it continues to fuel the suspicions of outsiders about illegal or immoral acts. Thus, the religion is threatened both by becoming too public and remaining too secret. As the religion becomes institutionalized, it faces losing the controls and benefits of the esoteric transmission of knowledge. If it remains secret, it suffers the harassments of civil authority in ignorance.

One example of this dilemma is the development of texts for the religion. Authoritative texts are public in that all may have access to them, and they become the means to maintain discipline against charlatans, criminals, or fools. Yet they obviate one of the signal benefits of the religion, the contextualization of the teachings in the face-to-face transmissions of initiation ceremonies. As the religion in the United States moves from strictly oral to some forms of written transmission, the issues of the authority of the texts become paramount. Until recently anyone seeking information on the tradition either had to commit to some level of initiation or had to rely exclusively on texts written by outsiders to the tradition. Recognizing the role that her books had begun to play as ritual texts, the late Cuban folklorist Lydia Cabrera wrote a Spanish-language primer with the imperative title *Koeko Iyawo*, or in English *Learn, Novice!* I have been flattered when a number of leaders have told me that they use *Santería: African Spirits in America* in instructing their English-speaking neophytes.

But the tradition is ready to move beyond outsiders' images of it, no matter how well intentioned they might be. Priests and priestesses are endeavoring to publish their own texts, both as practical guides for their own communities and as educational texts for outsiders. Notable among these is the work of Ysamur Flores, Julio Garcia, Babalorisha John Mason, Philip John Neimark, Oba Oseigeman Adefunmi of Oyotunje,

Cecilio Perez, Ernesto Pichardo, Miguel Ramos, and the Caribbean Cultural Center of New York. The boundaries between scholar and practitioner are also being explored in universities as academically trained participants are producing new texts and interpretations of the religion. Robin Evanchuck and Ysamur Flores at UCLA, David Brown at Emory University, George Brandon at CUNY, and Raul Canizares at the University of South Florida are actively presenting new and more thorough visions of the religion to the scholarly community.

With the emergence of texts, the demarcations among the communities practicing the religion become more apparent. Each community becomes committed not only to its own way of ritual practice but also to certain texts with their own terms of self-description and orthography. The very name *santería*, with its implications of dependence on the Roman Catholic idea of "saint," is rejected by many contemporary practitioners as trapping all discourse about the religion into discussions of syncretism and as overemphasizing the European elements of the tradition.

I chose the term *santería* because it was in use in the Spanish-speaking community I visited in New York. *Santería* is also the term used in the academic community I was joining, a usage given authority by the anthropological texts written in the middle decades of this century. If I were to be true to the new expressions of the religion, those being forged by the practitioners themselves, I might choose to speak of "the *orisha* tradition," or more simply "*orisha*," referring to the spirits that inspire the tradition.

Even these terms raise interesting issues of social linguistics and orthography. The word *orisha* comes from the Yoruba language of Africa and roughly translates as "spirit" in English. It is often rendered *òrìṣà* by those who know contemporary Yoruba in order to indicate the tonal quality of Yoruba vowels and variations in the Yoruba sibilants. These sounds are often anglicized by native English speakers and written as *orisha*, appearing this way in a number of texts including this one. Both the "ş" and "sh" sounds are foreign to Spanish speakers so most of the orthographies rendered in Spanish texts reproduce the word as *oricha*.

The differences of orthography become significant in the study of the tradition because they can indicate the different linguistic and cultural backgrounds of their writers and different attitudes about the past and future of the religion. Many practitioners of the tradition, especially those not of Cuban or Hispanic descent, are particularly concerned with the African origins of the religion and seek to reform the religion as closely as possible on contemporary Yoruba models. Air travel has made visits to Nigeria and Benin relatively available so that a number of priests and priestesses have received their initiation in Yorubaland. Because contemporary Yoruba religion and its Cuban expressions have undergone substantial changes since the time of the slave trade, there are many differences between the tradition brought to the United States by Cubans and that learned by recent visitors to Africa. These differences can be the source of friction between communities, some of whom seek to recover the purity of African practice, while others insist on the integrity of the changes to the religion carried out by slave and free ancestors in Cuba.

By calling this book *Santería*, I am revealing a certain attachment to the history of anthropological study, an interest in the development of the tradition as it has come from Cuba, and a concern with the importance of the Hispanic and Roman Catholic heritage in its development in diaspora. Yet I see the future of the religion in the United States becoming increasingly independent of all these influences. Practitioners are defining the tradition for themselves, there are fewer and fewer ties to Cuba, and the "sacred canopy" of Catholic civil relition is largely irrelevant in the United States. While this has a good deal to do with the efforts of leaders to learn from contemporary Yoruba teachers, I would argue that it is also a product of the influence of the North American values of secularism and religious pluralism.

American notions of religious commitment ask the believer to stand for one tradition among others in the context of a pluralistic society. I believe that this environment is important in motivating those committed to the *orishas* to proclaim this way of worship as their religion and forswear others. When many practitioners in North America speak of the Catholic elements of the tradition as a disguise for the true faith in the *orishas*, I wonder if this exclusivism would characterize the practitioners in Cuba of a generation ago. I argue in this book that the saints, at least as they were understood among the Cuban Americans that I knew, were not "disguises," but perhaps "masks" for the *orishas*. A mask, in Yoruba thought, is not a false front, but a complex relationship between two levels of experience, a symbolic, exoteric presentation of an esoteric reality. I think that the Roman Catholic tradition of saint veneration was maintained by the Cuban children of the *orishas* as a genuine, if less profound, level of participation in the complex mosaic of their religious experience. I would argue that the saints were masks which on the one hand disguised the identity of the bearers and on the other expressed them to the wider world.

Yet all this is changing in the United States. Perhaps the need for disguises is past, perhaps the public referents of the mask no longer resonate in the wider society. In any event the *orishas* are losing their Catholic forms in the United States and the name *santería*, with all its historical implications, will likely pass out of usage among the practitioners themselves. It remains for the priests and priestesses of the tradition to develop the texts to correct, educate, and, I hope, engage outsiders in appreciating the spiritual beauty that their tradition offers them.

The goal of this book is to provide a path for outsiders to an understanding of the tradition as it is experienced by insiders. I have attempted to present the religion as my teachers would want it presented. Noting the idealistic portrait that I have drawn, one critic has said that this book is a view of the religion as I would wish it to be, not as it really is. I take this criticism to heart, for in some ways it is true: the religion is full of credulous and venal people. Charlatans abound. People use ideas of spiritual power to intimidate and coerce others. I can only respond by noting that these abuses of trust are found in all communities. Given the centuries of disparagement of santeria in particular and of the cultural achievements of black people in general, I feel it my duty to present the religion in its best light. My teachers were knowledgeable and admirable people who were living with honesty and dignity in the harsh life of the Bronx. The basics of the tradition that they passed on to me were given subtle and complex nuances of meaning, the equal of anything that I had encountered in Western theologies.

It remains for me to express once again my thanks to the priests and priestesses who have taught me and to sing praise to the memory of Padrino, Ifa Morote.

Joseph M. Murphy
March 1992

NOTE

1. In June of 1993 the Supreme Court reversed the judgment of the lower courts and declared unconstitutional the Hialeah municipal ordinances banning "animal sacrifices." The mayor of Hialeah has said that the city will initiate no further actions against the church, and church leaders look forward to "institutionalizing the Santeria religion."

PREFACE TO THE 1988 EDITION

The research for this book was carried out over several years of visits to a santería community in Bronx, New York. The research technique is sometimes called by the unwieldy and even contradictory name of "participant observation." Using this method, I have supposedly participated in and observed scores of santería ceremonies. Yet I wonder now just how an observer participates and how a participant observes. The santeros that I met made it clear to me that, unless I abandoned the observation post of scholarly distance, I would never understand the mysteries of the *orishas*.

I have tried to respond to their demands for participation by keeping the scholarly apparatus to a minimum and by quoting only primary sources in the early chapters on santería's history. The endnotes provide for documentation in the secondary literature and point to resources for further research. A bibliography at the end of the book lists the most important studies of Yoruba religion and santería.

In the middle chapters, where I recount my own experiences with the santería community, I have tried to overcome the contradictions of participation and observation by writing in the first person. This abandoning of omniscience has meant taking certain liberties in recording times and places as well as concealing and changing names to ensure privacy. Still, I have tried very hard to record what was said to me in the context in which it was said. The dialogue has often been translated and edited to serve didactic functions, but I believe it accurately reproduces the setting and the sense of what was told me by many santeros.

Despite these efforts, I remain an observer and an outsider to the tradition. It is mine only when I can translate its wisdom into the language of my own experience. The book concludes with interpretation, Western and theological, of the meaning of this profound way of wisdom. What follows is thus at once an ethnography and a self-projection and so reflects the basic problem of participating and observing, of believing and interpreting.

Finally, my understanding of santería is limited by my level of initiation. Santería's wisdom becomes apparent only by long and dedicated progress through a series of ritual steps. My participation in santería ceremonies places me only at the very beginning of a process of learning that takes a lifetime. I ask experienced *olorishas* their indulgence in allowing their story to be told by an *aleyo*, a beginner.

I wish to thank Leonard Barrett, my professor and adviser, for pointing me toward the wonder of African religions; my *padrino*, Ifa Morote, and all the *olorishas* who have taught me; my parents, Richard and Mary, who have supported me in every way imaginable; my wife, Jane, who has listened to endless retellings of this story with grace and humor; and the *orishas*, who have blessed us all.

MODUPE LONO GBOGBO YIN

NOTE ON ORTHOGRAPHY

I have taken a number of liberties in anglicizing Yoruba and Lucumi words by dropping most accents and diacritical marks and by constructing plurals with the letter s. For readers who speak these languages, the words that have been reproduced are unambiguous in this context. For readers who do not, I am sure that these changes will make their reading much more agreeable.

Iba ara ago o
Moyuba
Iba ara ago o
Moyuba
Omo de ko ni
Iba ara ago o
Moyuba
Fe Eleggua Echu lona

Greetings O people
I bow to you
Greetings O people
I bow to you
I have come today
Greetings O people
I bow to you
Eleggua Eshu, move out of the way

INTRODUCTION

In a basement in the heart of the Bronx, a religious ceremony is coming to a close. Nearly one hundred people have come from all over the city to sing and dance for the gods of their ancestors. They are quiet now, and, in their midst, four old women dance together slowly. They wear white dresses and headties, and their brown faces shine calm and fine. They sway in a circle, and, though their backs are bent, their feet move in delicate rhythm. As they dance, they sing a song from Africa:

> *Olokun, Olokun*
> *Baba Baba Olokun*
> *Moyuba Baba Olokun.*

> Olokun, Owner of the Ocean
> Grandfather Olokun
> We bow before you father Olokun.

For a few moments, the mean streets outside vanish before a world of the spirit, a primordial Africa of the heart.

These people are called *omo-orishas*, children of the spirits. Their religion is an ancient one born in Africa, carried by slaves to the New World, and lovingly preserved through two hundred years of hardship. The religion has been brought to the Bronx by Cuban *omo-orishas* who came to New York with the great exodus of Cubans after the revolution of 1959. The women in white are priestesses of spirits called *orishas,* and they are praising Olokun, the *orisha* of sea depths who protected their ancestors on their terrible journey from Africa to the New World. They have brought their knowledge of the African mysteries to others in the city, Puerto Ricans and Dominicans, black Americans and Haitians, all in search of the wisdom of the mother continent.

The religion is often called *santería,* the way of the saints, a reminder of the religion's history of struggle and adaptation. When Africans were brought to Cuba and the other lands of the New World, they were forced to disguise their ancestral religion and to embrace the church of their captors. The founders of santería called their African gods *santos* (saints) and venerated them in churches according to the Roman rites. But, among themselves, they worshiped the saints with the songs and dances remembered from the motherland.

The necessity to hide the old religion from persecution has led to many misunderstandings among outsiders. Santería is confused with sensationalized images of sorcery fueled by newspaper headlines such as, "Blood Cults Spread through U.S." These images of sensuality and evil are little more than our society's cultural projections of repression, insecurity, and racial prejudice. While there are undoubtedly sinister uses for spiritual power, they are overwhelmed by the beauty and uplift that santería holds for its devotees. The religion offers a generous, supportive community, a refuge where people can meet together and enter a sacred world of possibility. The rituals of santería—dances and divinations, sacrifices and initiations—bring devotees to a spiritual family and to a world of the spirit where everything is poised and perfect.

I came to this world by what appeared to be chance. I was a graduate student in search of a dissertation topic. One day, a Cuban friend mentioned a grandmother who "goes to a medicine man in the Bronx." He took me to meet her, and she spoke of her *padrino,* her godfather, and the wonderful peace of mind that his spiritual guidance had given her. She asked the spirits if my spiritual path was open to instruction, and, receiving a positive response, she made arrangements to introduce me to the man who would become my Padrino, my godfather in the religion. It seemed to me that it was luck that brought me to the oldest and most respected priest of the religion in the United States. "There is no such thing as luck," Padrino told me, and it is the acceptance of this notion that is the first step in the way of the saints.

My path in this book is the narrow one between the demands of dispassionate scholarship and a loyalty to the believers' point of view. Most previous books on santería have been either social-scientific analyses or uncritical guides to ritual practice. This book is an attempt to balance the insights of observation and participation, of scholarship and experience. In order to present such an appreciation of santería, the book is divided into three parts. The first is historical, tracing the origins of santería in Africa and its transformation in Cuba. The second part tells the story of my own experience with santería through my visits to a particular community in New York. The third part steps back from this experience and looks at the significance of santería as a living expression of African heritage, as a focus of cultural resistance and pride, and, finally, as a world religion of beauty and power. What follows is the story of this religion called santería.

PART 1

1

AFRICA

This story of the spirit begins in Africa, among a nation of people called Yoruba in what is now known as Nigeria. The Yoruba were and are a great urban people who have lived in cities for at least one thousand years.[1] They have been master brass and iron smiths, weavers and dyers, and carvers of some of the finest sculpture arts in the world.[2] They achieved political importance in the seventeenth and eighteenth centuries as Yoruba trade routes spread over the whole of West Africa and the king of the city of Oyo took tribute from most of the kings of the Western Sudan.[3]

Perhaps greatest of all Yoruba achievements was the development of a subtle and complex religious way of life. Many scholars and artists have given us pictures of Yoruba religion, and this sketch owes something to each of them.[4] It assumes that the Yoruba religious vision is genuine and rooted in one peoples' experience of God.

The Yoruba call God Olodumare, the "owner of all destinies," the almighty, the ground of life.[5] Olodumare is the ultimate destiny of all creation; from him all existence comes forth, and to him it all returns. His breath is this force, this pulse of life and death. The Yoruba sing of Olodumare:

> Be there 1,400 divinities of the home
> Be there 1,200 divinities of the marketplace

Yet there is no one divinity to compare with Olodumare
Olodumare is the king unique.[6]

Olodumare is incarnated in the world as force, called
ashe. *Ashe* is the blood of cosmic life, the power of Olodumare
toward life, strength, and righteousness. *Ashe* is like a divine
current that finds many conductors of greater or lesser recep-
tivity. For the Yoruba, these channels have rhythms that can
be learned and used. What follows is a way to organize the
many different metaphors of divinity in Yoruba religion.[7] We
can speak of three basic approaches to a highly populated
spiritual world: the way of values through honoring ancestors;
the way of power through relationships with spiritual beings;
and the way of order through divination. Values, power, order—the ways of *ashe*.

VALUES—*ARA ORUN*

Ashe is present in the human line of continuity with the past.
Every generation owes its being to the one before it. Each
provides the conditions for the generation to follow. The
Yoruba venerate ancestors because they recognize that the
community of the present must look to the past for moral
example. The experience of the elders provides the precedents
and authority for juniors to grow in *ashe*. The Yoruba call the
ancestors *ara orun*, "people of heaven," and they symbolize
their presence among the living on earth in many ways. They
are in the litany of the names of forebears invoked at every
family ceremony, calling the departed to witness that the
living remain true to the old virtues.[8] They are in the beaded
crowns that veil the faces of Yoruba kings, reminding courtiers
that they are in the presence of a dynasty.[9]

Perhaps the most dramatic of all the appearances of the
ancestors is their annual return to the world of the living in
costumes of whirling cloth. In nearly every traditional Yoruba
town, the season of the yam harvest is celebrated by the
appearance of masked dancers in the streets called Egungun

who represent the *ara orun* by their unearthly costumes.[10] They are covered head to toe in swatches of bright, appliquéd cloth so that there is no indication of an ordinary mortal beneath. For a full week they appear at various points in the town in clusters of twos and threes. The Yoruba recognize a great variety of Egungun; some are clownish tricksters, others deadly serious. All hear petitions from the living that they will carry back to the ancestral community in heaven. Women frequently approach the mysterious figures to ask their favor in unlocking the mystery of generation and grant them children from heaven. Other women follow the dancers around the streets singing the praises of the departed and testifying to their generosity and efficacy. The atmosphere is one of joy and awe. John Pemberton heard women singing to the Egungun,

> Okin Elego-o-o-o [an Egungun]
> His children flow forth like palm wine
> Anumi's wife will never be barren.[11]

The Egungun can be as fierce as they are generous. They criticize the behavior of the living and hold them to the highest moral standards. They expose the bad blood and evil intentions harbored among neighbors. They are quick to bring supernatural punishments on sorcerers and witches who would undermine the moral authority of antiquity. The women sing,

> Ori-le-kee, my father.
> Rohum Jagbe. Famous king
> Le-kee. Father of witches.
> Arowosoju. I swear that I am not a witch.
> One who strikes terror like the snake
> Whoever sees the snake and does not flee, plays with
> death.[12]

The annual appearance of the Egungun whirling in the streets and alleys of Yoruba towns ensures the Yoruba of the continued guidance of the past and hope for the future.

There is another way that the ancestors are present in Yoruba life, and that is in the depths of the human soul. The Yoruba believe that every man and woman is a composite of visible and invisible properties integrated by a spiritual force called *ori*, "the head."[13] All the physical characteristics and mental dispositions of the individual have been "chosen" by the *ori* before the individual's birth. The Yoruba say that the *ori*, before being born in a body, kneels before Olodumare and chooses its destiny for its life on earth. This destiny is personified as *iwa*, character, and it is the development of *iwa pele*, good character, gentle character, which is the moral responsibility of every Yoruba man and woman. "*Iwa* is another name for religious devotion," says a Yoruba proverb.[14] This is the moral ground of devotion to the head, *ori*. The Yoruba praise their *ori*,

> If I have money,
> It is Ori who I will praise.
> My Ori, it is you.
> If I have children on earth,
> It is Ori whom I will praise.
> My Ori it is you.[15]

But the *ori* is more than just the individual soul; it is the very source of the individual and as such can be shared by other members of the individual's family, living or dead. Physical resemblances are thus evidence of a much deeper connection, a sharing of souls. This sharing of souls suggests that the Yoruba believe that there are only a finite number of *ori* in a constant process of transmigration between heaven and earth. The Yoruba show their belief in reincarnation by giving children such names as Babatunde, "Father-returns," and Yetunde, "Mother-returns." So, while the ancestors can be seen as living in peaceful compounds in heaven and returning as the otherworldly Egungun, they are also mystically present as the "heads" of the living.[16] They guide and admonish their children as forces from beyond or as conscience from within.

POWER—*ORISHA*

Alongside the moral *ashe* of the ancestors, the Yoruba find spiritual strength in relationships with a pantheon of spiritual beings called *orishas*. [17] The *orishas* are personifications of *ashe* that can be put at the disposal of human beings who honor them. The *orishas* came into the world at its beginning at the holy city Ile Ife, where they established such Yoruba arts and sciences as farming, hunting, smithing, and divination. Eventually, through their immense power and influence, they "passed through the earth" and became divine patrons of Yoruba life. [18] For some, they are the arts and sciences themselves. For every important Yoruba activity, there is an *orisha* whose power underlies it and whose mysteries will deepen it. Ogun, for example, is the patron of smiths who unlock the secrets of the earth and forge them into tools. Ogun can also be the force of iron itself, its *ashe*, which can be channeled into the peaceful arts of agriculture or the terrible ones of war. [19] Ogun is imagined as a dark warrior with bloodshot eyes. Praises to Ogun reflect his fierce strength:

> Ogun kills on the right and destroys on the right.
> Ogun kills on the left and destroys on the left.
> Ogun kills suddenly in the house and suddenly in the
> field.
> Ogun kills the child with the iron with which it plays.
> Ogun kills in silence. [20]

The complement to the hot power of Ogun is the cooling *ashe* of the *orisha* Oshun. [21] She is the patron of the river that bears her name and, so, cool water itself, which brings health and refreshment to her children. She offers the barren the joy of children in this praise poem:

> Brass and parrot feathers
> on a velvet skin.
> White cowrie shells

on black buttocks.
Her eyes sparkle in the forest,
like the sun on the river.
She is the wisdom of the forest
she is the wisdom of the river.
Where the doctor failed
she cures with fresh water.
Where medicine is impotent
she cures with cool water.
She cures the child
and does not charge the father.
She feeds the barren woman with honey
and her dry body swells up
like a juicy palm fruit.
Oh, how sweet
is the touch of child's hand![22]

As Ogun is the hard strength of iron, Oshun is the yielding force of water. Each is a different refraction of Olodumare's *ashe.*

Traditionally, the Yoruba recognize as many as 1,700 *orishas,* though only a few have achieved renown throughout the country. These great *orishas* are promulgated by organized priesthoods of men and women who have dedicated their lives to the service of a particular spirit. Any Yoruba city is honeycombed with shrines to the various *orishas* of the locality, each maintained by a priest or priestess. The shrines can be humble corners in ordinary household compounds or elaborate buildings attached to the palace of the town king. Often they are open groves on the outskirts of the town where the *orishas* like to receive offerings.[23]

The *orisha* Shango probably has more shrines than any other *orisha* since his worship was once connected to the royal house of Oyo. Long ago, Shango himself was an Alafin, or king, of Oyo renowned for his bravery, his swift justice, and his sorcery. Fearing this terrible combination of powers, the Oyo council overthrew him, and he withdrew into the forests, where, in despair he is said to have hanged himself.

But the king did not die. He became an *orisha* and now metes royal justice on wrongdoers through his fearsome thunderbolts, which fall all too often in tropical Yorubaland.

Human beings today can encounter Shango in the iconology of his shrines.[24] The finest Shango shrines are arranged like a royal court in miniature. At the periphery are wooden statues of courtiers, commissioned and donated to the shrine as ex-votos by those whose lives have been blessed by Shango. They are often delicate renderings of women suckling babies born through Shango's intercession or women cradling their breasts in supplication to the life force that Shango dispenses. These carved courtiers face the royal throne, a wooden mortar like those used in grinding grain. Yoruba kings sat on these ritual mortars to show that their authority both controlled and depended on the annual harvest.

Atop Shango's throne rests the most central symbol of his *ashe*, one or more meteorites, heavenly stones now on earth. They often sit in calabashes of water infused with special herbs to cool their lightning-hot *ashe*. At the foot or against the walls of the shrine are Shango's *oshes*, wooden scepters carved in the form of the double ax, special symbol of the thunder king. Shango's *oshe* splits the skies, raining lightning-fire on those in his path. His children sing of him:

> Fire in the eye, fire in the mouth, fire on the roof,
> You ride fire like a horse.[25]

Priests and priestesses of the *orishas* act as leaders of Yoruba worship. They undergo long and careful training in dance styles, prayer songs, and herbal healing.[26] A priest or priestess grows in *ashe* by his or her growing confidence in the mysteries of the *orishas*. By knowing how to make the *orisha's ashe* present for those who consult them, priests and priestesses contribute to the growth and health of the community.

The Yoruba express the presence of the *orishas* in dancing. The *orishas* are present in beautiful movement that can reveal the *orishas' ashe* in the complexity and nuance of rhythm.[27]

It is when the rhythms become hard indeed that the *orishas* may come to earth in their most dramatic form. They descend to "mount" their human children, and, like a rider takes command of a horse, they seize human bodies to dance among their children on earth. This possession by the spirit usually engulfs only trained mediums whose heads have been prepared to render this service to the community.[28] But the *orisha* may reach out with its ecstacy to anyone present in the spirit. In this way, the *orisha* puts out a call for new devotees.

A senior priest or priestess will generally take one or two students as novitiates in the mysteries of his or her patron *orisha*. For small services, he or she will instruct the neophyte in the long liturgical prayers that successfully invoke the spirits. Slowly, the student will learn the secret herbal medicines that can cure illness and deflect evil. From mere memorization, the student begins to learn nuances of herbal lore.[29] The herbs come to form a sacred way of classifying all of Yoruba experience, a kind of grammar of Yoruba religion that aligns the *ashe* of each *orisha* with its dances, prayer songs, drum rhythms, and icons.

When the novitiate is ready, he or she undergoes a rigorous nine-month isolation in order to be reborn in the spirit as an *omo-orisha*, a child of the *orisha*.

When one is initiated into the priesthood of the *orisha* Obatala, one takes on the characteristics of this serene deity. Omo Obatalas dress entirely in white and are held to the highest standards of purity and righteousness. The Yoruba say, "Their lives will be clear and pure like water drawn in the morning."[30] They avoid palm wine, red meat, and anything that might lead to passion or rash action. Obatala's children sing of him,

> He is patient.
> He is silent.
> Without anger he pronounces judgement.
> He is distant,
> but his eye rests on the town.

He kills the initiate
and rouses him to new life.[31]

Obatala is the perfect spiritual complement to Shango, and many Yoruba myths contrast them. One famous story tells of Shango, the fiery young king of Oyo, heedlessly imprisoning an old man who he thought has stolen his horse. The prisoner calmly waits until his identity is revealed as Obatala, the wise Oni of Ife. Abashed, Shango is forced to release the senior king. From the story, we can see the political claims of the senior kingdom of Ife and the wisdom of patience before youthful folly.[32]

The Yoruba show their deepening relationships with their *orishas* through sacrifice, *ebo*.[33] In gifts of animals and plants, human beings honor the *orishas* and dispose them to offer gifts in return. Life for life, *ashe* for *ashe*, humans grow in the divine exchange of energy. The *orishas* offer health, children, and wisdom; human beings render sacrifice and praise. Each needs the other, for, without the *ashe* of the *orishas*, human beings would despair of their God-given destiny and turn on themselves. And without the *ashe* of sacrifice, the *orishas* would wither and die. For they are not immortal; they depend on human beings for their life, their *ashe*. It is their worship that makes them strong, and, without the blood of sacrifice, they cannot fight for their children. The Yoruba recognize this interdependence in the proverb, "Where there is no man there is no divinity."[34]

Ogun and Oshun, Shango and Obatala, are only a few of the hundreds of *orishas* who offer life and hope to their devotees. Each offers a different road to wisdom and success, a different path of *ashe*.

ORDER—*IFA*

Perhaps the most reflective of the ways of *ashe* is that of Ifa, the path of divination.[35] Through Ifa the Yoruba can discern the will of Olodumare in the events of the world. Ifa reveals that in chaos there is order, in chance destiny.

Ifa is the name of a technique of divination held in great esteem by the Yoruba. It requires ten to fifteen years of arduous training to learn, and masters of the art are called *babalawos*, "fathers of the mystery." They are perhaps the most respected of all Yoruba priests, and the mystery they can reveal is Olodumare's destiny for all beings, human and *orisha*. The *babalawos* sing of Ifa,

> Ifa is the master of today.
> Ifa is the master of tomorrow.
> Ifa is the master of the day after tomorrow.
> To Ifa belong all the four days [of the Yoruba week] created by Oosa on earth.[36]

In the beginning, Olodumare gave the *orisha* Orunmila a flawless method of communication between himself and the *orishas* called Ifa. Through the patterns in the random fall of palm nuts from Orunmila's hands, Olodumare would reveal the precise destiny of anyone who sincerely asked. Orunmila knew the art of interpreting the nuts and taught it to his sixteen sons; they, in turn, passed it down to the *babalawos* who practice it today. There are many methods of Ifa: palm nuts, a chain of connected nut valves called an *opele*, or more simplified versions that depend on the fall of cowrie shells or kola nut valves.

Babalawos practice their art openly in market squares as well as in the courts of family compounds and royal palaces. They are generally senior men (women *babalawos* are very rare)[37] whose beaded jewelry and tools mark them as high priests.[38] They sit flat on the ground with legs outstretched, their tools before them. Querents approach, asking the *babalawo* to consult Ifa in order to learn the will of Olodumare as it touches their particular problem. Any problem great or small may propel a Yoruba to a *babalawo*: failures in conception, a lost lover, persistent bad luck, an upcoming journey. Through Ifa, the *babalawo* will give the querent a formula for action to meet and resolve the problem in the light of the will of Olodumare.

A typical session may begin in the shade of a market stall where a *babalawo* receives a young mother worried that her children seem overprone to sickness. Is this the will of God? Is there a spiritual problem of which these illnesses are symptoms? How can the problem be resolved?

She kneels before the Ifa tools and whispers her fears to a coin. This is the fee of the *orisha* Eshu, a mischievous trickster-*orisha* whose good will is necessary for the proper transmission of the message to Olodumare. If Eshu is satisfied, the *babalawo* will be permitted to keep the coin as part of his professional fee for his consultation. The *babalawo* now begins the process of determining the precise spiritual situation of the querent mother. Taking sixteen consecrated palm nuts in his left hand, he rapidly draws the bulk of them away with his right. He is trained in this maneuver to leave behind only one or two nuts remaining in his left hand. He does this eight times at each point leaving one or two nuts behind. The woman and the *babalawo* believe that it is purely a random process that determines whether one or two nuts remain on each occasion—random, but not chance. For, in the will of Olodumare, there is no such thing as chance. And, in what appears to be purest chance, the voice of the divine is clearest.

Ifa is linked to destiny through the symbolism of the number sixteen. Sixteen is the number of cosmos; it represents the primal order that issued from the unity of Olodumare. When the world was first created, it spread out from an original palm tree that stood at the center of the world at Ile-Ife. The palm had sixteen branches, which formed the four cardinal points and the sixteen original quarters of Ile-Ife. In political terms, Odudua, the first oni of Ife, fathered sixteen sons who founded the sixteen original kingdoms of the Yoruba. We have seen that Orunmila, the diviner *orisha*, taught the art of Ifa to his sixteen sons. Through the linked concepts of order, creation, and destiny, the number sixteen represents the variables of the human condition, the sixteen possible situations of human life. For the Yoruba, the sixteen principle signs are called *odu*, from each of which are drawn sixteen subordinate signs (*omo-odu*, "children of the *odu*"). These represent the sixteen essential life situations with sixteen possible variations each. This means 256 possible combinations or two to the eighth power. The goal of the *babalawo* is to arrive at the appropriate *odu* for the situation of his querent.

As each of the eight passes is made, the *babalawo* draws a corresponding figure in a special sawdust on a carved tray called *opon*. The result might look like this:

II   II

II   II

II   II

II   II

This figure, or *odu*, is called Oyeku Meji. It has fallen on this occasion, the *babalawo* says, because it was supposed to have fallen. What seems like chance is the breath of Olodumare. This *odu* is his answer to the woman's question of sick children.

Each *odu* is a recital of a set of poems (*ese*) that provide clues for the resolution of the problem. Master *babalawos* may know ten or more *ese* for each *odu* and display this enormous learning by being able to recite them from memory. The Yoruba scholar and *babalawo* Wande Abimbola translates one of the *ese* of the *odu* Oyeku Meji in this way:

You are Oyeku
I am also Oyeku
Daylight is just appearing in the skies
But people thought it was already morning.
Ifa divination was performed for Fish
Who was an offspring of the river bed.
Fish was told to perform sacrifice.
They told her that she would have many children,

But she was warned to perform sacrifice to prevent
    attacks of human beings.
She did not perform sacrifice.
She said it was not possible for enemies
To see her children at the bottom of the river.
She took her Ifa priests for liars,
She called Eshu a thief,
She looked fearfully to heaven as if she would never die.
She turned a deaf ear to the warning concerning
    sacrifice.
When human beings got up,
They took hoe, calabash, and sieve.
They dammed the river,
And started to drain off its water.
When there was no water left on top of Fish and her
    children,
Human beings took them,
And put them on top of pounded yam. [to eat]
It was the commandment of Eshu
Which prevented the complete annihilation of all
    species of
Fish from the earth.[39]

What does the mother of sick children make of this? A
story of a mother who does not honor Eshu—who boasts of
her invulnerability and disdain for the warnings of Ifa—is
destroyed by the community of human beings. It is only Eshu,
the wronged *orisha*, whose intercession prevents complete dis-
aster. The application of the mythic prototype of Fish to the
problem of sick children is discussed and decided together by
the *babalawo* and his querent.[40] She is counseled to sacrifice
to Eshu. Perhaps her childrens' illnesses are connected to
arrogance such as that of Fish. Eshu is often especially active
in puncturing spiritual pride by bringing misfortune to those
who forget humility or moderation. The woman is presented
with a moral precedent and a prescription for efficacious sacrifice. Diagnosis and treatment are divinely revealed, bringing
everyday problems into the context of the will of Olodumare.

19

Each of the 256 *odu* reveals an archetypal situation that was resolved in the mythic past through sacrifice to an *orisha*. In the thousands of Ifa poems, the *orishas* are organized into a community of spirits whose *ashe* can be brought to bear on the problems of individual men and women in need. In this way, Ifa and the *babalawo* priesthood are responsible for directing the cults of all the *orishas* by leading querents to them. Nearly all the sacrifices of Yoruba religion are offered to the *orishas* as a result of divination. Ifa structures *orisha* worship; the randomness of the system ensures that all the *orishas* are duly venerated. Through Ifa, the balance of the sacrificial relationship between heaven and earth is maintained, for Ifa provides human beings with information about their place in the world, their destiny, and what the gods require of them. Ifa and the ceremonial life that it generates constitute the organizing principle of the Yoruba religious vision. It is a view that finds human destiny rooted in the breath of God Almighty. Nothing happens by chance, and it is the duty of human beings to recognize this mystery—to grow in *ashe* by respecting elders, by honoring *orishas*, and by attuning themselves to the unfolding mystery of divine destiny.

It is this vision that hundreds of thousands of Yoruba men and women brought with them when they were taken across the Atlantic to work as slaves. This vision sustained them through one of history's darkest hours, and it is today sparking a spiritual renewal in the streets of New York.

2

CUBA

In the late eighteenth and early nineteenth centuries, the Yoruba waged a series of disastrous wars with their neighbors and among themselves.[1] In 1796, the weak Alafin of Oyo, Awole, was overthrown by a coalition of lesser chiefs who could not hold together the disintegrating empire. Vassal states proclaimed their independence, and a series of alliances and counteralliances pitted the Yoruba against each other for much of the next century. In 1804, the charismatic Fulani leader Usuman Dan Fodio rallied his people in an Islamic jihad that overthrew the Hausa leadership of northern Nigeria and expanded to confront the pagan Yoruba to the south. Finally, encouraged by the disarray of the Alafin's forces, the Fon kingdom of Dahomey invaded from the west. These internal and external blows led to the downfall of the Oyo empire and the enslavement of hundreds of thousands of its Yoruba subjects. The American missionary Thomas Bowen correctly assessed the situation in 1851: "It is true, that these wars, except for those of the abominable Dahomy, were not generally commenced for the sake of capturing slaves; but once begun, for political reasons, they have commonly been nourished by the slave trade."[2]

Bowen witnessed terrible devastation among the Egba branch of the Yoruba people, who he said were enslaved in "multitudes" destined for Cuba and Brazil. Between 1820 and 1840, the majority of slaves shipped from the ports of the

Bight of Benin were Yoruba: victims of fratricide, Dahomean expansion, the Fulani jihad, and, most of all, the insatiable demands of the planters of the New World.

At the same time that the Oyo empire was crumbling, events in Europe and the Americas would have grave consequences for the Yoruba people. In 1762, the English Lord Albemarle brought the Seven Years War to the Caribbean by capturing the Spanish port of Havana. The English occupied the city only for a year, but the economic consequences of their victory transformed Cuban society.[3] Once the sole prerogative of the Spanish crown, Cuban trade was now opened to foreign markets. Europeans had developed a passion for sugared foods, and, with the successful revolt of Haitian slaves in 1791, Cuba stood alone to profit from a huge infusion of foreign capital. The island economy of small farms and harbor industries was overwhelmed by the clearing of the largest sugar plantations in the world.

Hundreds of new sugar mills required thousands of laborers to plant, harvest, refine, and ship the "white gold." The work was so arduous, the conditions so wretched, and the owners so profit obsessed that free labor could not be contracted to work in the mills. The demand for slaves was enormous. Thus was set in motion a process that would bring Africans to the New World on a scale never before imagined. Hundreds of thousands of these were Yoruba, and the story of the Yoruba spirit now moves to Cuba.

The trade in slaves from Africa was nothing new to Europeans. From the time of Herodotus, black Africans were a familiar presence in the Mediterranean world.[4] After the Islamic conquest of Iberia in the eighth century, black Africans appeared at Spanish courts as ambassadors and traders and sometimes as slaves. In the centuries-long struggle for the reconquest of the peninsula, Christian warriors would seize the households of vanquished Moors and enslave the inhabitants, black, brown, or white. By the time of the Spanish discovery of the Americas, Seville held nearly 15,000 slaves, many of African descent.[5] Many of these accompanied the earliest voyages of exploration and fought bravely in the great and terrible conquest of the native civilizations. In the early ports of the Caribbean, slaves of African descent worked as stevedores and launderers, tailors and smiths.[6]

The story is often told that Africans came to be taken directly from Africa due to Father Bartolome Las Casas's concern to protect the Indians from the rapacity of Spanish overlords. In the early decades of the sixteenth century, Las Casas witnessed horrible cruelties inflicted on the Indians by the conquistadors. He wrote a polemic imploring the king to interfere on the Indians' behalf and allow colonists to import Afro-Spaniards to work in the mines and farms of the New World. Las Casas could never have imagined, much less condoned, the enormous suffering that would come from the African slave trade.[7] Nevertheless, a trade began in the sixteenth century that would build relentlessly until, by slavery's end in Brazil in 1888, nearly ten million African men and women had made the middle passage.[8]

Africans from Senegal to Madagascar were caught in this whirlwind, and they came to Charleston and Havana, Port au Prince and Bahia. And they were not just Africans, but Ashanti and Mende, Ibo, baKongo and Ga. As the nineteenth century dawned, more and more of them were Yoruba. Statistics will not convey the "shock of enslavement,"[9] the imprints of chains and beatings, the destroyed lives and the early deaths. The slaves were brought into a world of hatred and greed; yet they survived and built within it a spiritual world of beauty and order. It is this world we will look to in the chapters to come.

SLAVE SOCIETY IN CUBA

No one knows how many Yoruba slaves were brought to Cuba during the 350-year slave period. Good estimates of the total number of Africans taken to Cuba range from 527,828[10] to 702,000.[11] We do know that a large number of these were Yoruba and baKongo, for their influence is everywhere in Cuban music, dance, and religion.

Most of the Yoruba who survived the middle passage found themselves enslaved on the new sugar plantations.[12] The big mills or *ingenios* were hellish places where labor was cheap and life short. Absentee owners found it more profitable to work slaves to death and buy "fresh" recruits from Africa than to maintain a slave community. The rhythms of sugar production could be brutal, alternating periods of cultivation with frantic periods of harvest when slaves could work as many as twenty hours a day. The slave poet Juan Francisco Manzano wrote these lines, translated by abolitionist Robert Madden in the late 1830s:

> With twenty hours of unremitting toil
> Twelve in the field and eight to boil
> Or grind the cane—believe me few grow old
> But life is cheap, and sugar, Sir—is gold.[13]

Despite the institutional terrorism of the *ingenios*, Africans resisted their enslavement at every turn. Though the slave owners often justified slavery by theories of the natural servility of Africans, the specter of the Haitian revolution was never far from their minds. They lived in constant fear that the island would become "africanized."[14] The great scholar of Afro-Cuban culture, Fernando Ortiz, reports that there were nine major uprisings reported in the eighteenth century. In 1812 alone, slaves fought in four serious revolts on *ingenios* and one in Havana itself. In 1825, a revolt in Mantanzas ended with twenty-four farms sacked and burned and fifty-eight dead—fifteen whites and forty-three blacks.[15]

Slaves resisted their enslavement by destroying machinery and burning cane fields. They used African medicines to keep a master or to kill him.[16] They often killed themselves—a gesture of despair, but also one of resistance, for they chose it believing that they would be borne back to Africa.[17]

Not the least of the methods of resistance was escape. Early in the island's history, African slaves had escaped into the hills to establish communities with other *cimarrónes*, or "wild men," as they were called. These communities lived by hunting, gathering, and raiding the plantations of the lowlands. They were a constant source of irritation to the planters and of communication and escape for the slaves. In the eighteenth and nineteenth centuries, the *cimarrónes* established fortified settlements known as *palenques* with their own social institutions and traditions.[18]

Little is known of *palenque* life, although the names that have come down to us such as Bumba and Maluala suggest Kongo ethnic influences. If they follow the pattern of other runaway communities, they provided important opportunities for African religious traditions to survive and adapt to the New World. In the nineteenth century, numerous expeditions were launched against the *apalencados*, with little success. They were gradually displaced as more of the island came under cultivation and the wars of independence absorbed them into the island's revolutionary conflicts.

Though fewer slaves lived in the cities of Cuba than in the countryside, their cultural impact was greater.[19] In the cities, slaves could make lives for themselves that would have been impossible on the *ingenios*. In the cities, they had opportunities to learn trades, and they frequently worked for wages. They became shipbuilders and wheelwrights, blacksmiths and stevedores. Havana newspapers carried advertisements placed by slaves offering their skills for hire.[20]

Even more important than this economic mobility was the possibility for full legal freedom that urban life offered. The civil and religious laws of Catholic Cuba guaranteed slaves rights of private property, inviolable marriage, and personal security. Though these rights were often ignored in practice, they could be better safeguarded in the cities by the presence of civil and diocesan authorities charged with protecting them. First among these rights was that of *coartación*, by which a slave could legally purchase his or her freedom from a master for an agreed and published price. Though the slave owners in general resisted this practice, the substantial population of free people of color throughout Cuba's history indicated that *coartados* were not rare.[21]

In the mid-nineteenth century, free people of color, *gente de color*, formed over one-third of the black population of the island and nearly one-sixth of the total population. By comparison, in Virginia, free blacks made up about one-ninth of the black population and one-thirty-second of the total population of the state.[22] The *gente de color* of Cuba were concentrated in the cities, where they dominated a wide variety of trades and services. In a census of 1871, it was shown that free blacks comprised the majority of Havana's masons, tailors, teamsters, stonecutters, and many other skills and trades.

These opportunities to live a relatively independent life gave urban slaves and *gente de color* the hope necessary to create a vibrant cultural life. They forged the time and space to meet with their fellows, establish their own households, raise families, and learn trades. And only in the cities could they meet regularly with their brothers and sisters to celebrate the old ways and teach them to their children. When the Yoruba poured into Havana in the early nineteenth century, they found harshness and bitter injustice, but they also found each other. Slowly, they replanted the ways of *ashe* in a new world, meeting to honor the *orishas* and finding order and hope in the breath of Olodumare.

SLAVE RELIGION IN CUBA

The Yoruba men and women who came to Havana in the nineteenth century found a world both strange and familiar. Their masters must have seemed an alien caste apart, remote overlords who looked like monkeys and behaved like witches. The world was brutal and hostile and only the strongest survived. But there were refuges within it, points of contact with the old world that made the new one less savage. The Cuban sun still brought forth Olodumare's life, the forests and glades offered the same cooling herbs, and, if one were lucky, one found countrymen who spoke the old language and remembered the *orishas*.

The Yoruba were quick to establish a strong community in Havana. They came to be called "Lucumi" after their way of greeting each other, *oluku mi*, "my friend."[23] They formed guilds and dance halls, taverns and fraternities, where they would dance the old dances. More than ever they needed the *orishas* and their ways of power, and they found ingenious ways of keeping them alive. This story of survival involved an unlikely partnership between the *orishas* and the Roman Catholic church.

The Spanish brought Africans not only into a way of work but also into a way of life. To justify the terrible sufferings of slave life, Spanish law insisted that slaves be baptized as Roman Catholics as a condition of their legal entry into the Indies. Spanish jurists argued that a life of servitude was a small price to pay for the opportunity of eternal life with Christ. Royal decrees repeatedly emphasized the necessity of baptizing and catechizing African slaves. The Leyes de Indias state in specific terms the duties of church and state toward the spiritual welfare of the Africans:

> We order and command to all those persons
> who have Slaves, Negroes and Mulattoes, that
> they send them to the Church or Monastery at
> the hour which the Prelate has designated, and
> there the Christian Doctrine be taught to them;
> and the Archbishops and Bishops of our Indies
> have very particular care for their conversion
> and endoctrination, in order that they live
> Christianly, and they give to it the same order
> and care that is prepared and entrusted by the
> laws of this Book for the Conversion and Endoc-
> trination of the Indians; so that they be in-
> structed in our Holy Roman Catholic Faith,
> living in the service of God our Master.[24]

The slave code of 1789 reiterated the message: "All owners of slaves, of whatever class and condition that they are, must instruct them in the principles of the Catholic religion and in the true necessities in order that they be baptized within one year of their residence in my dominions."[25]

Some priests attempted to carry out this mission with energy and sincerity. In seventeenth-century Cartegena, the Jesuits Alonso de Sandoval and Pedro Claver dedicated their lives to bringing Christian compassion to the sick and despondent among the newly landed Africans.[26] In Cuba, Felix Varela and Antonio Maria Claret strove for the abolition of slavery and genuine catechesis for the slaves.[27] But these shining examples of Christian altruism were overwhelmed by the entrenched greed of the slaveholding caste and the indifference of their fellow clerics.

Though the church failed to bring Christian justice to Cuba, it still had profound influence on slave life. As Christians, however nominal, Afro-Cubans found themselves enmeshed in a Catholic folk culture with their own important part to play.

Only the Catholic church was capable of representing the stratified and heterogenous society of colonial Cuba as a unity. Island society was a maze of classes, castes, and racial and ethnic groups. When the ports of Spain poured out Castillians and Andalusians, Galicians and Basques, Cuba created a new mosaic of Spanish ethnicity.[28] Those born in this new society were called *criollos*, Creoles. In Creole society, African ethnicity was taken as a matter of course. Slaves born in Africa were called *negros de nación*, that is, of a distinct African "nation" or ethnic group. Fernando Ortiz listed over one hundred African ethnic groups known in Cuba. Though a much smaller number would be able to preserve their ethnic identity as the nineteenth century continued, by the century's end some fourteen African *naciónes* had preserved their ethnic sense of themselves in Havana social clubs.[29]

These clubs, called *cabildos*, are the key to the survival of Yoruba religion in Cuba. And it survived as a direct result of the policies of the Cuban Catholic church. Although the church probably did not intend to keep the *orishas* alive, it did so by recognizing the diversities of African ethnicity as much as those of Spain. As *negros de nación*, the Lucumi found their place in this creole mosaic and so kept alive their language, culture, and religion.

The *cabildos* were societies of blacks, slave and free, organized by the church for the purpose of religious instruction and mutual aid. Each was made up of Afro-Cubans of the same *nación*. The church hoped that, by encouraging African ethnic organizations, it might find it easier to Christianize their members. As always, motives were mixed. By Christianizing Afro-Cubans, the church enforced the mores of a repressive society and controlled or channeled the creative life of Afro-Cubans into socially acceptable directions. Yet, by supporting the Christian status of Afro-Cubans, the church opened up legal opportunities and spiritual hopes that were seriously resented by the ruling caste.

For their members, the *cabildos* functioned as societies for mutual aid and as social clubs for entertainment and religious devotion. As mutual aid societies, the *cabildos* provided for the old and infirm. They arranged elaborate funerals for their dead. They also dedicated a portion of their dues for a fund to allow slave members to purchase their freedom as *coartados*. The church often acted as agent for the slaves in these negotiations as well as treasurer of *cabildo* funds. Some Cubans attribute the origin of the famous Havana lottery to the *cabildos'* fund-raising efforts to purchase their brothers' and sisters' freedom.

Fernando Ortiz, in his study of the old *cabildos*, tells us that they were justly famous for their dances. He notes a succession of laws designed to limit the ebullience of the *cabildo* dances. A law of 1835 reads: "The *cabildos* and dances of the blacks are not to be celebrated except on specific holidays and at the borders of the city, from ten to twelve in the morning and from three in the afternoon until evening prayers."[30] The dances celebrated in the *cabildos* were of African origin, each *nación* dancing in its own style. The by-laws of the Cabildo Arara Maguno state specifically: "The *cabildo* will give *fiestas* every holiday in the style of its *nación*, that is to say an African dance, prohibiting the interference of the drum rhythms not of their *nación*."[31]

29

Nowhere was the Africanness of Cuba recognized more clearly than in the great religious festivals of Epiphany, Carnival, Holy Week, and Corpus Christi. The liturgical cycle of the Catholic year offered Afro-Cubans the opportunity to inject their styles of celebration into the public festivities. On the great days, the *cabildos* came out into the streets, bringing their songs and dances into the plazas where all Cuba could join in.

They marched in processions bearing the banners and images of their *nación*. But the priests had done their job, for above all the masks and rhythms were the images of their patron saints. As early as 1839, the Lucumi had established themselves in the Cabildo Africano Lucumi under the advocation of Saint Barbara. On her feast day, 4 December, the Lucumi danced in the Havana streets under her image and flags emblazoned in scarlet and white.[32] When the *cabildo* was reorganized in 1891, its stated object was mutual aid in cases of sickness and death. At all festival days, the Lucumi would hold African dances "known by the names of their drums," and they prohibited all but Lucumi rhythms.[33] From this *cabildo* and others like it, the music, dances, and religious practices of the Yoruba were preserved—because of, but also in spite of, the efforts of the Catholic church.

The greatest feast of all for the Afro-Cuban population was the celebration of the Epiphany, or *día de reyes*.[34] It became their special day because of the legend of the black magus Melchior who came from Africa to adore the Christ child. Afro-Cubans found their role in Catholic society by identifying with this African presence in Christian folklore. On the *día de reyes*, they brought an African flavor to the celebration of the Christian feast.

The festivities began before dawn, when drumbeats could be heard throughout Havana, ringing from the various *cabildos*. Then, in full dress of feathers and mirrors, many masked and bedecked with bells, the marchers formed under their captains in the central square. Spectators crowded the balconies of the city as the dancers paraded the streets toward the palace of the captain-general. A nineteenth-century observer described the display as follows:

> As they were leaving the Palace in order to leave room for the others there marched in perfect order Congos and Lucumis with their great sombreros of feathers, vests with blue stripes and pants of red percal; Araras with their cheeks covered with scars cut with red-hot iron, bedecked with shells and the teeth of dogs and alligators, beads strung of bone and glass and their dancers had wrapped around their waists a big hoop covered with raffia; Mandingas very elegant with their wide trousers, short jackets and turbans of blue or red silk edged with marabu; and so many others, finally, with difficult names and fanciful clothes that were not adorned entirely in the African style, but reformed or modified by civilized influence.[35]

They marched down the broad boulevards to the palace of the captain-general, where he would review them from his balcony. Then, as the day and night wore on, they would dance their ways back through narrow, shuttered lanes to the *cabildos* to celebrate until dawn. Anyone bold enough to walk the streets late at night would come on small clusters of dancers whirling their way home or on to another party.

The carnival dances, loosely harnessed to the veneration of the saints, became the primary way for the Lucumi to be both Catholic and African. It was the way that they could show that they were important members of Cuban society while still celebrating their African vision.

SANTERÍA EMERGING

In the New World, the Yoruba were forced into a new religious system of pervasive power. This new tradition shaped their

31

lives, and their native vision of the world was gradually adapted to complement and reflect the Catholic worldview. A new bilingual tradition emerged, at once a resistance to Catholic oppression and an accommodation to Catholic values. It came to be called santería, the way of the saints, because the devotions to the *orishas* were carried out beneath the images of the Catholic saints. What may have once begun as a subterfuge, an attempt to fool Catholic observers while preserving the ways of the *orishas*, became a genuine universal religious vision in which a Catholic saint and a Lucumi *orisha* were seen as different manifestations of the same spiritual entity. As the Yoruba had become Lucumi in Cuba, so the Yoruba religious vision had become santería, an attempt to honor the gods of Africa in the land of the Catholic saints.

From the *cabildos*, several ethnically distinct Afro-Cuban religions emerged with more or less fidelity to their African past. The Efik of the Niger delta established the Abakua society, often called *ñañigos*.[36] Various Kongo peoples created the traditions called *nganga*, *mayombe*, and *palo monte*.[37] The Fon people, perhaps by way of Haitian immigrants, founded the various Arara cults. In his remarkable autobiography, Esteban Montejo talks of his impressions of the Afro-Cuban religions on several plantations where he worked as a slave in the nineteenth century. He tells us,

> I knew of two African religions in the barracoons: the Lucumi and the Congolese. The Congolese was the more important. It was well known at the Flor de Sagua [an *ingenio*] because their magic men used to put spells on people and get possession of them, and their practice of soothsaying won them the confidence of all the slaves. . . .
> The difference between the Congolese and the Lucumi was that the former solved problems while the latter told the future. This they did with *diloggunes* which are round, white shells from Africa with mystery inside. . . .

The Congolese were more involved with witchcraft than the Lucumi, who had more to do with the saints and with God. The Lucumi liked rising early with the strength of the morning and looking up into the sky and saying prayers and sprinkling water on the ground. The Lucumi were at it when you least expected it.[38]

We have seen that in the cities these Lucumi traditions were institutionalized in the *cabildos*. After independence and the end of the established church, the *cabildos* were reformulated specifically as communities called *reglas* after the regulations of *cabildo* life. The ethnic *cabildos* became semi-underground cults, each identified as a different *regla*. Sometimes santería is called *la regla de ocha*, the rule of the *orishas*.[39]

As the *reglas* established themselves in the early years of the twentieth century, their identity began to rest less on the ethnic descent of their members and more on the spiritual path that they followed. Fewer and fewer Afro-Cubans could claim birth in Africa, and most members of the *reglas* were *criollos*, Spanish-speaking natives of Cuba. The *reglas* had kept African ethnic distinctions alive, but their membership became increasingly open to all blacks, people of color, and, ultimately, whites whom the *orishas* might choose. One became a member of *la regla de ocha* or santería not by African descent but by cultic initiation.

The participation of these non-Lucumi initiates became common after independence, but there had been whites in black religious fraternities for a long time. The Cuban folklorist Lydia Cabrera, in her definitive study of the Abakua society, found records of white Spanish and Creole members at the dawn of the nineteenth century.[40]

The Abakua, or *ñañigos* as they were popularly called, were probably the most famous of Afro-Cuban *reglas*. Because of the secrecy of their rites and organization, they became identified in the middle-class mind with political subversion and gangsterism, of which they apparently were not entirely innocent. White children were raised with the terror that, if they were not good, *ñañigos* would come to take them away. During the first American occupation of the island (1898–1902), the *ñañigos* became the focus for a great deal of white paranoia, resulting in the supression of all the Afro-Cuban religions. Today much of the white Cuban population still associates the African traditions of the island with *ñañiguismo* and this with witchcraft and ritual murder.

Though the *ñañigos* did indeed form a gangster element of Havana's Afro-Cuban underworld in the early years of this century, it was not their Africanity that accounted for their brutality. Speaking of the bloodshed of Cuba's wars of independence, Esteban Montejo says, "It was like what happened here in the districts of Havana—Jesús María, Belén, Manglar—when the *ñañigos* set about each other in the African way. It was just the same. And you can't say it's because they were savages, because the whites who went in for *ñañiguismo* did the same."[41]

It is interesting that white attitudes toward the Africanity of Cuban culture were often shaped in childhood. Like the white children of the Uncle Remus stories of North American folklore, many white Cubans were raised by black nannies called *tatas*, who told the children of the mysterious world of the African gods. These fairy tales of the *orishas* and *ngangas*, together with the dread of the *ñañigos*, made African culture a kind of children's culture for many middle-class whites: a kind of folklore like elves, gnomes, and flying reindeer for their North American counterparts. As the new century of independence dawned, most white Cubans tended to see the African religions as quaint folklore told by illiterate *tatas* that was exploited by bandits such as the *ñañigos*.

Despite setbacks and prejudice in the political realm, Afro-Cubans sparked a great artistic movement in twentieth-century Cuba. Rather than shrugging off Africanness as either quaint or barbarous, Cuban writers such as Alejo Carpentier and Nicolas Guillen discovered a reservoir of cultural vitality in African-inspired music, dance, and poetry.[42] *Afrocubanisma* was born as a reaction to the naive progressivism and scientism of the pre–world war generation of independent Cubans. It was not, in this sense, truly a black movement, but a move-ment of black and white artists extolling what they believed to be a purer, nobler primitivity of the Afro-Cuban people. Like the European cubist painters and intellectuals in the mode of Spengler, the Afrocubanists rejected Western culture as decadent and artificial, and they sought to reexperience the assumed sensuality and emotional primitivism of the African.

The movement had run its course by the 1950s, ex-hausting the romance of exoticism and noble savagery, but it is through the movement that Cuba's interest in its own Af-ricanity was awakened and encouraged. The greatest of all recorders of Afro-Cuban life, Lydia Cabrera, was led to her work by European and Cuban intellectuals. It was primarily these artists who transformed much of Cuba's attitude of sus-picion toward Afro-Cuban culture into enthusiastic pride.

Finally, the movement created a literature of protest that has pitted the national values of Cuba against European and North American imperialism. The administration of Fidel Castro has built on this tradition in its national arts programs, but it has found itself in a difficult position. While extolling the independence and heroic resistance of its black popula-tion, the party has been forced to condemn the religious forms in which this protest has been carried out. Afro-Cuban reli-gion, although the primary vehicle of Afro-Cuban culture, has been officially relegated to museums, such as that at Gua-nabacoa. It remains to be seen how the cults will coexist with socialism.

Since the Cuban revolution of 1959, over one million Cubans of all backgrounds have left the island as political exiles. Among them were *santeros*, priests and priestesses of santería, who have established the way of the *orishas* in Puerto Rico, Venezuela, and particularly the American cities of Miami and New York. Once again, the *orishas* have been carried to a new land, and, once again, they are adapting and growing. Now that we have seen how deep the roots run—how Africa is the source of a people's pride, strength, and wisdom—we can begin to see their ceremonies and celebrations with new eyes.

PART 2

3

BOTÁNICA

If we would walk along the streets of any Hispanic neighborhood in New York, wedged between the busy groceries and newsstands we might see small retail stores called *botánicas*. To the uninitiated, their merchandise must look mysterious indeed: candles and beads, herbs and oils, cauldrons and crockery, and plaster statues of Catholic saints. Yet, for those who know their meaning, each of these items has a part to play in santería, the religion of the *orishas* in New York. Santería came to New York in the heads and hearts of Cuban emigrants, who came in waves after the revolution of 1959. It has prospered here, bringing growing numbers of Puerto Rican and black Americans into the way of the *orishas*. If we enter a *botánica*, we can get our first taste of this ancient African spiritual path in modern America.

This particular *botánica* is called La Caridad del Cobré and is found in the middle of a bustling Cuban neighborhood in the Bronx. In its picture window is a huge, life-sized statue of its patron, La Caridad del Cobré, the Virgin of Charity, Cuba's patron saint.[1]

At the dawn of the seventeenth century, Caridad appeared to humble fishermen and left them her holy image, which came to be enshrined at the town of Cobré at Cuba's eastern tip. Today her plaster image reveals a beautiful dark lady in perfect repose, crowned and holding a wise royal child. At her feet are the three fishermen, awestruck, hands clasped in adoration.

In the *botánica*'s window, Caridad is attended by a number of smaller statues of the important saints and virgins of Cuban folk piety—the dark Lady of Regla, crippled Saint Lazarus on his crutches, regal Saint Barbara with crown and sword.

But these are not only Catholic saints. To the initiated, they are just the public faces of more puissant and mysterious spirits, the *orishas*. The Lady of Regla is the Catholic face of Yemaya, lovely mother of the seas. Saint Lazarus is a public way of representing Babaluaye, the *orisha* of disease and healing. Saint Barbara is Shango, the great thunder king in the guise of a woman. And Caridad, the beautiful patroness, is Oshun, the sweet river goddess.

Some might see these Catholic images as disguises for the *orishas*, ways to preserve a secret tradition while pretending to practice another. It is true that secrecy has been vital to preserve the integrity of the tradition and protect it from the intolerance of bigots. Prejudice and oppression have taught the children of the *orishas* to be prudent in how they present their soul life to outsiders. Still, thoughtful devotees maintain that the Catholic saints are not disguises for the *orishas* but rather personae. They say that the saints are *caminos*, "ways" of the *orishas*, ways that the *orishas* manifest themselves to the Catholic world. Just as the Catholic church believes that the Virgin Mary manifests herself in different ways to different cultures, so these *santeros* have sought a universal vision of the *orishas*. For them, the *orishas* are capable of appearing to ordinary Catholics as pallid white saints and to *santeros* as the invisible forces of *ashe*.

The window scene of the *botánica* is reminiscent of the courtly serenity of the Yoruba temple, but, once we go inside the store, we are overwhelmed by a riot of merchandise for sale. Shelves and glass cases are crammed full of religious articles. One large case is devoted entirely to necklaces of brightly colored beads, each coded to a particular *orisha:* yellow or gold for Oshun, blue and white for Yemaya, pure white for Obatala, red and white for Shango. The beads themselves are cheap plastic, but some are finely strung with meticulous attention to numerical patterns. Each *orisha* manifests in different *caminos,* and the patterns must reflect which *caminos* the devotee wishes to invoke.

In fact, everything in the *botánica* is color and number coded to the *orishas.* Spiritual work done with Oshun, for example, should be done in fives and with the color yellow. In order to focus her life-giving *ashe* on their problems, devotees will light for her five yellow candles, offer her five yellow cakes, and wear yellow beads in various groupings of five, depending on her *camino.* These are her mystical coordinates that put her *ashe* to work for her human children. A complete chart of the *orishas* is given on pages 42 and 43.[2]

Piled high in unlikely corners are large crockery tureens in a variety of colors. These are *soperas,* great lidded bowls that will contain the most fundamental symbol of the *orishas'* presence—their holy stones.

In so many myths of the *orishas,* we are told that they left the primordial community of Ile-Ife by descending into the earth. All that remained of their presence were stones, still resonating with their *ashe.* Devotees can find these *orisha* stones among ordinary ones if they can learn to listen carefully enough. For the *orisha* stones are alive with the *orisha's ashe.* They are most likely to be found in the element most expressive of their force—ocean stones for Yemaya, river pebbles for Oshun, meteorites for the thunder king Shango.

The stones can answer that they are alive with an *orisha's ashe* by means of a number of oracles derived from Yoruba Ifa. The fall of coconut or cowrie shells, the patterns of Ifa chains or palm nuts, can be interpreted to listen to the stones' deep voice. If the stones are indeed alive, they are to be collected in a *sopera* whose color represents that *orisha.* There they are venerated as the *fundamentos* of the *orisha,* the most fundamental, tangible representation of the *orisha* on earth.

As embodiments of the *orishas,* the stones must be treated as the living things that they are, and so they are lovingly bathed in cooling herbs, cleaned and oiled, and fed with the blood of animals.[3]

Orisha	Saint	Principle	Number	Color
Agayu	Christopher	fatherhood	9	green, red, & yellow
Babaluaye	Lazarus	illness	17 or 13	black or light blue
Eleggua	Nino de Atocha, Anthony of Padua	way-opener, messenger, trickster	3	red & black
Ibeji	Cosmus & Damien	children	2	those of Oshun & Shango
Inle	Rafael	medicine	7	green
Obatala	Mercedes	clarity	8	white
Ogun	Peter, Santiago	iron	7	green & black
Olokun	Regla	profundity	7	blue & white
Orula	Francis	wisdom, destiny	16	green & yellow
Osanyin	Joseph	herbs	3	green
Oshosi	Norbert	hunt/ protection	7	lavender & black or blue & orange
Oshun	Caridad	eros	5	yellow
Oya	Candelaria	death	9	maroon, red, or brown
Shango	Barbara	force	4 or 6	red & white
Yemaya	Regla	maternity	7	blue & white

Foods	Dance Posture	Emblem
fish, meat	long paces, carries children	oshé
tobacco, rum, doves, hens	infirm, lame	crutches, reeds, & cowries
white chicken, rooster, opossum, rum	buffoonery	hooked staff
—	children's play	twins
—	fishing	leaves, earth
♀ goats, pigeons	calm reality	whiteness, fly whisk
♂ roosters, dogs	bellicose	iron
rooster, spiced rum	seas	shell
chicken, dove	dances through Oshun	ifa
rodents	does not dance	leaves, forest
doves, rum, guinea hens	hunting calls	bow & arrow
♀ white hen, goat, sheep	coquette	fan, gold, peacock feather
only fowl, hens, doves	bacchanal, storm	lance
♂ rooster, sheep, goat, pig, bull	aggression, violent acrobatics	oshé
duck, turtle, goat	smooth or raging seas	fan shell

The *orishas,* like all living things, must eat. Few aspects of the way of the saints is more misunderstood than blood sacrifice. To outsiders, it often appears as the essence of primitivity, for some romantically authentic, to others revolting and barbarous. But it is really none of these things. It is a way to show the relationship and interdependence of living things.

Animals die so that human beings may live. Urbanites forget the source of their food, that their consumption of beef or chicken—even vegetables—requires the death of living things. All are related by delicate exchanges and balances of nature that make human life possible. In santería, sacrificial animals are never slaughtered cruelly or wantonly. The cuts are quick and clean, and their flesh is eaten by all at the great feasts. Their blood is offered to the *orishas* to show human beings their dependence on the world outside them and to give back to the invisible world something of what it gives to the visible. *Santeros* are naturally reluctant to discuss animal sacrifices with outsiders, and we must be patient if we are to learn more.

In the apartments of New York, these blood offerings require containers like the *soperas.* They hold the fundamental stone symbols of the *orishas,* they contain the sacrifices that are offered through them, and they conceal the sacred stones from the eyes of the profane.

As befits a king, Shango has his own kind of *sopera,* the *batea Shango,* always in wood and always elevated on a wooden mortar stool, the *pilón. Santeros* in New York have not forgotten Shango's shrines and the Yoruba equation of kingly power and fertility. And they have remembered Shango's dispute with Ogun, the blacksmith, so that all Shango's tools are of wood, especially his mighty *oshe,* the double-headed ax. We can see a variety of *oshes* in the *botánica.* Some are just crude ax shapes sawn from plywood, but others are delicate and decorated with tribal marks like their Yoruba prototypes.

When the meaning of the *soperas* and *bateas* becomes clear, we might notice on a shelf behind the counter a neat

row of little iron cauldrons no more than six inches high.
They are fire blackened with rounded bottoms perched on
three nubby legs. These will contain the *fundamentos*, the
fundamental symbols, of Ogun, miniature tools of the blacksmith's forge—an anvil, a rake, a hoe, a pick, a machete, a
spade, a pike, a sledge. Like the stones of the other *orishas*,
Ogun's tools are worked from the ore of the earth and receive
warming blood and cooling herbs. They are the medium
through which Ogun eats and works.

As a warrior *orisha*, Ogun's tools are also weapons of war.
Ogun fights for his children, and his tools must be in a constant
state of preparedness. They must be kept clean and well oiled
with palm oil. As the devotee grows in the religion, he or she
will learn how to use the tools as symbolic medicines to protect
against those who would do the devotee harm.

Beside Ogun's tools, the *botánica* has placed a stylized
bow and arrow wrought in iron, the fundamental symbol of
Oshosi, *orisha* of the hunt. Oshosi and Ogun are natural com-
panions, for both blaze paths through the forest and both are
knowledgeable about the secret powers of forest leaves. These
rugged, independent *orishas* walk together to protect the devotee from the jungle of dangers outside one's doorstep. Life
continues to be hard for the children of the *orishas*. New York's
dangers may not be those of Cuban slavery, but devotees still
need spiritual toughness to battle the hard world of the inner
city.

Ogun and Oshosi often walk with a third companion,
whose fundamental symbols are usually kept out of sight. Yet,
in a small case on the floor behind the counter, a sharp observer may see a cluster of small cones of grey concrete about
three inches high. Embedded in the concrete in the right
places are three small cowrie shells forming a pair of eyes and
a jagged, open mouth. These are rough busts of the *orisha*
Eleggua, opener of the paths of *ashe*.

Eleggua is the Cuban Lucumi name for Eshu, perhaps
derived from the Western Yoruba praise name Eshu-Elegba.[4]

Like his African counterpart, New York's Eleggua is a powerful, restless observer of the human condition. He is sometimes imagined as a little boy, a mischievous trickster fond of dangerous practical jokes. At other times, he is a serious monitor of human behavior, gatekeeper to the world of the *orishas* and messenger to Olodumare.

These images of trickster and monitor of conscience have prompted some devotees to find correspondences between Eleggua and the Christian idea of the Devil. Purists are quick to point out that Eleggua is not a force for evil like the Dantean Prince of Darkness lurking in Christian mythology. Yet Eleggua does resemble the Advocate of the book of Job, restlessly overturning human complacency.[5]

Eleggua's conical shape is a convenience to contain medicines that energize the concrete to convey hard, aggressive *ashe.* He is properly placed in the home of a devotee at the threshold, and, together with the other warrior *orishas,* Ogun and Oshosi, he guards the door against intrusive forces from the jungle beyond.

The concrete Elegguas in the *botánica* are hollow and inert, waiting for an herbalist's touch to transform them into the *orisha* at the threshold, who opens the way to his devotees and closes the door against a hostile world.

In a long glass case next to the beads is the real focus of the *botánica* that gives the store its name. This is the botanical merchandise of packets and dried clusters of herbs sacred to the *orishas;* herbs to make holy infusions, to focus and channel *ashe. Santeros* find that herbs impregnated with *ashe* have amazing powers to cure body and soul.[6] Blessed in ceremonies to Obatala, elecampane can cure bronchitis. Consecrated by Shango, sarsaparilla will alleviate nervous disorders. Oshun's river fern can be infused into bathwater to relax the mind and turn the evil intentions of others back on them.

Herbs can be made to energize spiritual medicines. Bits and pieces of small symbolic objects can be tied together and infused with the appropriate herbs to protect the wearer from evil influence. *Santeros* call these protective bundles *niche osain,* medicines sacred to Osanyin, *orisha* of forest leaves.

Osanyin is imagined as a leaf man, with one leg like a long stem.[7] He hides in the forest and yields his secrets only to those who know where to look. This relationship with Osanyin made the old *santeros* true botanists, some with staggering knowledge of thousands of plants and their properties. Osanyin's fundamental symbol is a short staff called an *osun*.[8] We see them now on the upper-most shelf of the *botánica*, six-inch steel dowels, surmounted by a small cup rimmed with little bells on chains. Fixed to the lid of each cup is a two-inch steel rooster. The cup will contain *ashe*-filled herbal medicines; the rooster plays on Yoruba associations between birds and magical powers as well as the sacrificial blood that releases the herbs' power.

Herbs can be medicines for the *orishas* as well as for human beings. The *orishas* are volatile spirits who can have both benign and wrathful incarnations. A devotee's love of an *orisha* is always tempered by a respect for a much greater force. Shango wields blazing thunderbolts; Oshun is a passionate woman who cannot be scorned. As the red blood of sacrifices warms and empowers the *orishas,* green herbs can cool their overheated *ashe* when their stones are bathed in fresh, herbal water.

Herbs keep the *orishas* happy and serene and keep their human children healthy in body and soul. They are at the heart of the religion, and the herbmaster is its most vital office. Above everything else, the herbs are what make the religion work, and their properties and symbolic meanings are the most closely guarded secrets of the way of the *orishas*.[9]

The *botánica* is nothing if not catholic in its technology of spiritual work. Many patrons will supplement their work with the *orishas* with other systems of spirituality. The entire back wall of the store is devoted to shelves of twelve-inch votive candles in all the colors of the rainbow. *Santeros* have learned from Catholic liturgies that the powers of saints can be focused on the problems of the living by showing the pure flame of devotion at the feet of their images. Many *santeros* will supplement the African style of devotions to the *orishas* with more orthodox Catholic veneration of their saintly counterparts. The *botánica* does a brisk business in the rosaries, Bibles, prayer books, scapulars, medals, and statues familiar to Catholic folk piety everywhere.

Some patrons of the *botánica* are said to "cross" (i.e., to supplement) the way of the *orishas* with spiritualist séances. The writings of the nineteenth-century French spiritualist Alain Kardec continue to be enormously popular in the Hispanic world.[10] In the spiritualist tradition of *mesa blanca*, the world of European mediumship and that of the *orishas* has been brought together ("crossed"). The *botánica* carries large supplies of florida water, the universal solvent and conductor of these spirits.[11]

These more European devotions are sometimes derided by purists faithful to the African origin of santería. They especially deplore the mass-produced good-luck charms and amulets that the *botánica* offers to the credulous—lucky number books, anti-jinx spells, get-rich-quick pendants. The herbs have even become modernized into aerosol sprays of doubtful content. Distanced from the ritual acts that can truly energize an object spiritually, these objects only alienate the devotee from the healing work of preparation. It is training and devotion that make a *santero*, say the purists, and only that knowledge and love can further *ashe*.

Most *botánicas* sell lottery tickets, and patrons sometimes buy one for the *orishas*, hoping the spirits will bring the lucky number to pass. At several stations in the Botánica de la Caridad del Cobré, small Plexiglas boxes have been fixed before statues of the *orishas*, and they are usually filled with coins, bills, and lottery tickets.

Despite its commercialism, the Botánica de la Caridad del Cobré offers the genuine *santero* a refuge from a much colder world outside. Thrust into the most urban world imaginable, the *botánica* preserves something of the forest, the pure and wild realm of Osanyin, and so the world of the *orishas* in New York.

4

ILE

There are over one hundred *botánicas* scattered around the five boroughs and Bergen County. We can only guess how many *santeros* it takes to support them. The *botánica*, like the saints, is only the public face of the world of the *orishas* in New York. It is open to all who find it, but the community that supports it is more difficult for outsiders to know. Members have had to be suspicious for so long, prejudice has buried the tradition so deeply, that they will not often open it to strangers.

Santeros live for the *orishas* and to help those who seek the aid of the *orishas*. They are not interested in explaining or justifying the religion to the disinterested observer. If we wish to go further, we must find a personal reason beyond curiosity. We must be willing to give something of ourselves for the *orishas* to respond.

I do not yet know what inspires me in my own search into the world of the *orishas*. It is partly academic research and partly the romance of a strange world. But there is something further, something in the depth of commitment I see in the eyes of *santeros*, something in the depth of the rhythms of the drums, that I recognize in myself. It is as if I am being called.

Perhaps the owner at La Caridad del Cobré senses this willingness in me even if I cannot yet name it. He tells me that there is one *santero*, a true *babalawo* living in New York, who will speak with me. He is Oba Ifa Morote, the founder of santería in the city. Everyone knows Padrino, "Godfather," I am told. As I enter more deeply into the world of santería, this certainly seems to be true.[1]

He was born in Cuba in 1903 and grew up with the presence of the *orishas* everywhere. At his birth, the Ifa oracle proclaimed that he would be a *babalawo*, a "father of mystery." In 1944, he "made Ifa," that is, mastered the art and received the tools of Ifa divination from Quintin Lecon, one of the most respected *babalawos* on the island.

But he grew restless with life in Havana and came to New York in 1946. After a period of struggle and poverty, his knowledge and wisdom gradually attracted the first *ile*, or house of the *orishas*, in New York. It became apparent to all the seekers in El Barrio or Spanish Harlem that Padrino knew more of the *orishas* than anyone and that he was uninterested in exploiting his knowledge for gain.

In 1964, he organized a drum ceremony for Shango at the old Casa Carmen in Harlem that attracted three thousand people, including Latin music stars Julio Collazo and Machito. As his reputation grew with his *ile*, he came to be called on to preside at initiations throughout the Hispanic world. Since the 1950s, he has been flown to nearly every South American and Caribbean country to be godfather to a new initiate. By his own estimate, he has some six thousand godchildren.

All this activity prompts some *santeros* to describe Padrino as a "businessman." An *ile* on such a scale, they argue, must be too impersonal, supervision of initiates too infrequent, to assure their grasp of the tradition. There is no question that Padrino blends his kindness with shrewdness. He has had to be very careful leading and advising so many people on a spiritual path so misunderstood by so many. Yet, if he is a businessman, he is not a rich one. His house is small and plain. He supported his family as a postman until his retirement. He turns down commissions that he suspects, and he always allows the *orishas* to dictate his fees for his services.

There is no better time to meet Padrino and to get a sense of his *ile* than on the feast day of his patron Ifa, celebrated on the day of Ifa's Catholic counterpart Francis of Assisi, 4 October. On this day, all Padrino's godchildren are asked to come to his house to pay their respects to Ifa. I speak to Padrino on the telephone and ask if I can come. "Sure," he says in colloquial English, "all my godchildren will be there. You can learn a lot."

Ifa's feast day is 4 October because the Cuban Lucumi were forced to adapt their liturgical calendar to the cycle of the Roman church. Saint Francis's beaded rosary reminded them of Ifa's divining chain, the *opele,* so they honored Ifa on Saint Francis's day. Today most *santeros* see Saint Francis as a Catholic manifestation or *camino* of Ifa and, thus, essentially the same spirit.

Padrino's Bronx neighborhood is tough by most standards, but the small, semidetached brick houses are well kept. I enter his house by a side door to the basement, now crammed with people of every description imaginable. These are the *babalawo's* godchildren, at this moment some three hundred strong in the basement of a city duplex—three hundred out of several thousand.

Moving forward through the throng, I am brought to the ritual focus of the house. There, in a recess on the other side of the basement, Ifa, the patron of the house, sits arrayed in glory. The walls and ceiling are draped in green and gold satin, forming a luxurious tent for a cylinder some two feet high placed atop a three-foot pedestal. The cylinder is also hung with green and gold, this time silk brocade, concealing the *fundamentos,* the sacred instruments of Ifa.

This tabernacle is surrounded by hundreds of offerings: candles flicker, flowers perfume the close air, and mounds of yams and coconuts radiate out from Ifa in state. During the course of the day, godchildren have been passing through the house; each bringing the traditional gift to Ifa, a large Cuban yam, two candles, and two fresh coconuts. It is now only early evening, and there must be nearly five hundred yams piled before the shrine.

Squarely before the pedestal is a huge, tiered cake, iced in green and gold, with the words *Maferefun Orula* drawn in dark green gelatin around the base. Orula or Orunmila is another personal name of Ifa. *Maferefun* is a ritual expression of thanksgiving. Thus, "Thanks be to Orula," "Thanks be to Ifa."

Each devotee prostrates himself or herself before the shrine and recites the ritual greeting to Ifa, *Iboru iboya ibochiche*, "May Ifa accept the sacrifice." The devotees then turn to Padrino and prostrate before him not only because he is an elder but also because he is a *babalawo,* he carries Ifa in his person. Padrino ritually touches their shoulder blades and blesses them in Lucumi. The devotees then embrace Padrino in turn, and their respect and joy at greeting the great man on his day are apparent.

Padrino is a tall man with smooth light brown skin now grown soft with age. He has a full head of iron-grey hair that he wears short in almost military fashion. His eyes are large and liquid and betray a sad weariness. He is both hard and soft, and his godchildren respond to him with both great respect and great affection.

I try my best at a prostration before him, and he laughs gently. "Welcome to my *ile,* my house," he says. "Look around. Listen to what my godchildren say about the religion. Maybe later I'll show you the *orishas.* "

I thank him and begin to edge my way around the crowded house. I find old and young people, Afro-Americans, Puerto Ricans, and Cubans. Little children run by at play; teenagers sit together, some boisterous, some withdrawn. Very old women are leaning on canes and on each other. There seem to be about four women for every man.

Many people are unknown to each other, but all are tied by the ceremonial kinship of the *ile*. The *ile* is like a great family in which everyone is related, not by blood, but by initiation. In order to receive the various initiations into the *ile*, one must be "born" into them. Godmothers and godfathers "give birth" to initiates, who, in turn, when they have acquired enough knowledge and *ashe,* can give birth to godchildren of their own. Every santería *ile* is a complex hierarchy of initiates grouped into families of godchildren.

Padrino is godfather to nearly all the people present today because he has given them his special protection as a *babalawo*. Most of the younger people here have received their warrior *orishas* and their *osun* from him, special fundamental symbols and symbols of entry into his *ile*.

The people at Padrino's house are bound by the obligations of a spiritual family. They owe their godparents total filial respect, and they must treat each other as brothers and sisters. As youth must venerate age, they owe respect to those initiated before them, and they must show patience and generosity to those who follow. Thus, a devotee's duties are set by his or her "spiritual age," a sixty-year-old man initiated four years ago honors and obeys a thirty-year-old of ten year's initiation.

As I survey the crowd, I see small signs of these relationships. Men and women prostrate themselves at others' feet. Some scurry to fetch glasses of water for their godparents. A few can be seen carefully fanning their elders. Some, however, move through the room with unquestionable authority.

One is Efundare. She is a slight, bent old lady, but her brown eyes are quick and irreverent. Born in Puerto Rico in 1903, she came to the United States in 1927. She tells us that Indian spirits of the Puerto Rican hills have guided her since childhood, and her work with them has made her one of the foremost spiritists in New York. She answered the call of the *orishas* in 1958, and she "made Obatala" in Guanabacoa, Cuba. She now maintains her own *ile* of many godchildren of all races and backgrounds. She has even traveled to Nigeria and taken some of the most distinguished titles and initiations in Oshogbo, the home of Oshun. She is one of the firmest bridges among the many sides of santería, African, Cuban, Puerto Rican, Afro-American.

Another senior *santera* of great abilities is Obashalewa, Cuban-born daughter of Shango. She is a small, heavy woman, nearly sixty, with delicate hands and a penetrating gaze. She has lived in the United States since 1952, but she returned to Cuba in 1958 to "make Shango." She returned to New York that year and became the first *santera* to "make saints" in the city rather than sending candidates to Cuba as all had done before her. Since the early 1960s, she has been godmother to thirty-one *santeros*—Americans, Puerto Ricans, and Cubans.

Obashalewa has also distinguished herself as a spokeswoman for the tradition before courts of law, where *santeros* have appeared as defendants in cases brought against them by the American Society for the Prevention of Cruelty to Animals (ASPCA). She argues publicly, as all *santeros* will privately, that the sacrificial animals of santería are killed quickly and cleanly, that they are always eaten, and that they are the ordinary fowl and four-legged animals available preslaughtered in most supermarkets. The ASPCA has wisely avoided debating the relative cruelty of methods of animal slaughter and initiated prosecutions for violations of zoning ordinances when *santeros* bring farm animals into city apartments. The cases against the *santeros* are solid ones, but there are important constitutional issues at stake, and *santeros* see ASPCA raids as another chapter in the religion's long history of harrassment. Obashalewa continues to defend them, and, with Shango behind her, she is a formidable power indeed.

As I move back from these senior priestesses, I fall into conversation with Olatutu, a black American man in his fifties. As the priestesses radiate strength and worldly wisdom, Olatutu is small and gentle and only newly initiated into the way of the *orishas*. But his story is that of many other seekers who find themselves in Padrino's *ile*. Olatutu is a self-taught scholar of the mystical traditions of the world. He has found in santería a grand synthesis of his reading in Egyptology and his participation in Moorish Science and Masonry. For him, the *orishas* are the purest expression of the primordial African wisdom that gave birth not only to Egypt and Ethiopia but to human life itself in the Rift Valley. His conversation glides easily from reincarnation to the Bible to astrology. All, he argues, are *orisha* inspired. He is a soft-spoken man, far from an elder in the tradition, but his linkage between the way of the *orishas* and the greatness of the African past is a powerful force in bringing Americans of African descent to the call of the *orishas*.

More confident is big Oyeyemi, a black American son of Obatala and indefatigable researcher of the tradition. For ten years, he has been working with Yoruba-speaking residents of New York, translating Lucumi texts and working for harmony and understanding among the various branches of the tradition. Furthering this work is Oshagbemi, a young Puerto Rican woman who has organized international conferences bringing priests and priestesses of the tradition from Cuba and Brazil, Haiti and Trinidad, to meet with their Yoruba counterparts in Nigeria. These younger *santeros* represent a new generation that is carefully documenting the tradition and proudly bringing it before the whole world.

Besides Padrino, the busiest person in the *ile* is surely his wife. She is a big Cuban woman with dark-dyed hair and smooth white skin. She moves about the crowd, receiving her own godchildren graciously, being polite to senior priestesses, and playing hostess to the throng. She is a daughter of Oshun as befits the wife of a *babalawo*, and, like that *orisha*, she can be charming or terrible as the occasion demands. She is a good deal younger than Padrino—his second wife, in fact—and she has come to the responsibilities and prestige of his huge *ile* by marriage. Some of the elders are reluctant to recognize her authority, but she now has many godchildren of her own. I will call her Madrina, Godmother, but I will recognize that most members of the *ile* have their own godmothers to whom they owe their first allegiance.

Madrina and Padrino have a number of grown children and little grandchildren, and, together with Padrino's children and grandchildren by his first wife, the house is always full of affectionate and busy family life. Even the littlest of these is a full initiate in the religion and commands the respect of spiritual juniors. Today the grandchildren are having a wonderful time with the attentions of such a huge and doting audience.

On 4 October the house is so full of people that it is difficult to imagine it on ordinary days. Yet, as I look around carefully, I can see that each room has a special part to play in the maintenance of the *ile*. It is home to a continual cycle of feasts, ceremonies, and initiations. It provides a place for the manufacture of the tools and adornments of the *orishas* and a room for consultations with the oracle, Ifa. The small duplex in the Bronx is a complete *ile*—a great extended family, a home for the *orishas*, and a center for the celebration of their *ashe*.

The basement room that enshrines Ifa in October will display other *orishas* throughout the year. Each *orisha* appears in glory on the feast day of his or her Catholic counterpart: Shango on Barbara's 4 December; Oshun on the Virgin's 8 September; Babaluaye on Lazarus's 17 December. Anniversaries of initiation are celebrated with a full display of all the *orishas'* regalia. Each time, the shrine room is draped with rich cloths in the appropriate colors. The *soperas* that contain the sacred stones are hung with sumptuous altar cloths, and the floor is arrayed with the *orisha's* favorite flowers, fruits, and cakes. In a prosperous *ile*, this regalia can be fine indeed and the sight breathtaking.[2]

The shrine of the sacred stones also acts as a throne room for new initiates, who, like the stones, are also vessels of the *orishas* and so sit in state on the day of their spiritual rebirth. When they receive the *orisha* in initiation, their "heads" become *fundamentos*, fundamental symbols of the *orisha's* presence, and so they too appear in silks and satins surrounded by the regalia of their patron *orisha*.

Some of the materials for santería initiations can be purchased in an ordinary department store. Others can be found in a *botánica*. But some must be made by the hands of a *madrina* or *padrino*. If we look away from the shrine area into the corners of the basement, we find that Madrina has a sewing area for the huge job of stitching the cloths and clothes of santería ceremony. Beside the sewing machine are shelves of glass jars and cases containing thousands of beads. Several unfinished *collares de mazo* are on her desk, giant versions of the single-string necklaces found in the *botánica*. When finished, each will contain hundreds of strands and weigh nearly five pounds.

Padrino also has a work area for the preparation of the warrior *orishas*, Eleggua, Ogun, and Oshosi. As Madrina prepares the intricate and soft adornments of the *orishas*, Padrino forges the hard fundamentals—Eleggua's concrete head, Oshosi's bow and arrow, and Ogun's iron tools. His workbench is essentially a New York version of Ogun's forge, where the metal tools of the guardians are made.

The central area of the basement is the *ile igbodu*, the African grove of the *orishas* brought into the heart of the city. The Yoruba often celebrated the *orishas* in groves, cleared areas between town and bush. Rather than erect cathedrals, they danced with the *orishas* in the open air, at a point midway between the known and the unknown. New York will not accommodate this tradition of the *igbodu*, and so a somewhat cramped area of Padrino's basement must serve. Today the area is full of milling people, but at another time it will hold drummers and whirling dancers. In the far corner, a huge stove waits for those ceremonies of sacrifice, when animal offerings will be dressed and cooked by priestesses and eaten in communion by all present.

Before leaving the *igbodu*, I almost overlook a small niche in the wall serving as a shrine to the *egun*, the deceased members of the *ile*. Their presence is symbolized by seven glasses of water, crosses, and a rosary, reminding us of the Catholic and spiritist influence on the santería cult of the dead. Lining the walls of the niche are photographs and drawings of the deceased, flanked by fresh flowers. The water in the glasses is fresh and clean, and the attention to the shrine reminds the faithful that the dead continue to be a part of the lives of the living. The *eguns* do not eat like the *orishas*.

Thus, their cult is much like the Catholic cult of the dead, and the afterlife is explained in Catholic terms of heaven, hell, and purgatory.

As I am musing on these objects and recognizing things that I have read about, Padrino comes up to me. "So you want to learn about the religion?" he asks. "Have you been reading any books?" I tell him of Ortiz and Cabrera. "Yes, yes, good, good," he says, a little impatiently, "but if you are really going to understand you're going to have to listen as well as read."

He takes me upstairs to the living quarters of the duplex. The house is furnished simply and neatly in bright pastels. The style is open and airy, more like a house in the tropics than New York. With only a few Catholic statues and holy pictures in sight, nothing would indicate to the outsider that the home is the religious center that it is except for one room off the top of the basement stairs. Padrino leads me into his consulting room and private shrine to the *orishas*.

The room is some twelve by fifteen feet and dominated by a near life size plaster statue of Jesus, the Sacred Heart with golden hair and scarlet cape. Surrounding this startling figure are literally hundreds of objects symbolic of the *orishas*.

"Do you know the name of the *orishas*?" Padrino asks. "Then who is that?"

I see the distinctive *pilón*, Shango's royal mortar stool, and, atop it, all in wood, is Shango's *sopera*, painted in symmetrical blocks of red and white. Leaning against the *batea* are Shango's tools—a short club completely sheathed in red and white beads and a simple wooden ax.

"Good, good," says Padrino. "Well, have a look around, take your time, pay attention. I've got to get back to my godchildren now but I want you to come back next week and we'll read Ifa for you. Okay?"

Once again, I thank Padrino and then begin my inspection of this extraordinary room.[3] Everywhere there are fruits and sweets of every description—melons and coconuts, cakes large and small. Bottles of soda and beer are displayed everywhere for the *orishas'* pleasure. Several of the *orishas' soperas* are raised on pedestals and clothed in altar cloths of satin and silk brocade. Each *sopera* is flanked by its *orisha*'s special emblem—Oshun's peacock fan, Obatala's white horse-tail whisk. The "fly whisk," or *iruke*, is a Yoruba symbol of royalty, and this one is extraordinarily fine. Its handle is nearly eight inches long, completely encrusted with white beads in elaborate cross patterns.

Beyond Shango's throne are the emblems of Oshosi, the hunter. Bulging out of an iron cauldron are deer horns, a real bow and arrow, and a safer version of their modern equivalent, toy guns. The fundamentals of the Ibeji, the divine twin children of Shango and Osun, are contained in two tiny covered jars, and two identical dolls represent them.

Next to them, two metal oxen pull a plow on a miniature farm, complete with fences and *bohío*, the beloved country shack of Cuban folklore. This is the shrine of Orisha Oko, the farm *orisha*, who furthers the fertility of crops and human beings. Offerings of yams and sweet potatoes line his miniature field, and a coconut, painted half red, half white, is his fundamental symbol.

In the far corner, Saint Lazarus-Babaluaye has his sick house of wood, a miniature building some two feet tall with little windows and an opening door. It s adorned with burlap, straw, and cowries, and two miniature crutches lean against its sides.

Since Padrino's home is the center of a great *ile* and the home of experienced *santeros*, the fundamentals symbols and adornments of the *orishas* have overflowed to occupy an entire room. The altars and shrines reflect a lifetime acquiring beautiful and consecrated objects to be placed before the *orisha*'s fundamentals. The sewing and beadwork require hundreds of hours of devoted attention and have been strengthened by the *ashe* of hundreds of ceremonies. In fact, any object that strikes the attention of the devotee, which reminds him or her of an *orisha*, can be consecrated to serve in the *orisha*'s shrine.

Many objects symbolize pacts with the *orishas*, ex-votos in thanks for the *orishas*' help and success in solving a particular problem. There may be small boats to thank an *orisha* for a safe journey or a doll to celebrate a departed ancestor or the birth of a longed-for child.

In a great *ile* such as Padrino's, these objects number in the hundreds, and their maintenance requires full-time devotion and attention. In ordinary santería homes, the fundamentals, ex-votos, and ritual entourage can often be contained in a shelved cabinet called a *canastillero*. Although it cannot contain all the objects of the shrine, there is a massive wooden *canastillero* in Padrino's room. Perhaps the stones are stored here on ordinary, nonfestive days.

In other homes, *canastilleros* can be as elaborate or simple as the means and attention of the devotee permits. Some are silk lined with scores of objects flanking expensive *soperas* of fine bone china. Others are spartan affairs of unfinished wood with just the *soperas* and primary tools of the *orishas* to adorn them. The *canastillero* has the advantage of closing doors, and many non*santeros* would be surprised to know that the great cabinet in a friend's living room contains the presence of the gods of Africa.

The shelves of the *canastillero* can serve as a way of ranking the *orishas*. Often Obatala, the "great *orisha*" and wise old king, is given place of honor on the top shelf, although some *santeros* will place their particular patron *orisha* there. Some *orishas* are ritually excluded from the *canastillero* shrine. The warriors Eleggua, Ogun, and Oshosi are placed at the threshold of the house. Shango must sit on his regal mortar. The herbal messenger, Osun, in his bird staff, is frequently elevated over all, protecting the life of the devotee and poised in flight to God. Each *ile* develops its own rules (*reglas*) in the shrine display and in the order of invocation of the *orishas*. Yet finally, the shrine takes the shape of the devotee's own relationship with the gods, growing larger, perhaps richer, but always deeper as he or she learns to give and receive.

In Padrino's *ile*, this private shrine room is also a place for consultations with his patron *orisha*, Ifa. Although the huge display of *orisha* objects commands attention, on the other side of the room is a small table and two chairs where

Padrino works his greatest service to the *orishas* and his fellow human beings. This is the consulting room of Ifa, where Padrino brings the wisdom of Africa to bear on the problems of her descendants in New York. I must return to hear it.

As I descend the stair back to the basement shrine, I know that I will be coming back to Padrino's next week as he asked.

5

IFA

When we watch Padrino in his consulting room, we learn so much of the history of Yoruba religion in the New World. We learn that master *babalawos* must have been passengers on the slave ships to Cuba. And they must have had extraordinary dedication to teaching their art in order to pass it on so that it would flourish in such complete form in New York nearly two centuries later. Amid the harsh world of Cuban slavery, *babalawos* must have found places to establish their Ifa practices. They must have found communities to support and consult them, and there must have been willing apprentices with the time and energy for the difficult task of learning the *ese* verses.

A *babalawo* must have at his memory's command the entire language of the *orishas:* thousands of *ese* divination verses, hundreds of prayers, songs, and praise names of the *orishas.* When slavery shattered the complex interrelationships of Yoruba religion, the *babalawo* became the focus for its reconstruction in the New World. In him was the knowledge to conduct every santería ceremony and to organize the proper herbs, foods, and sacrifices and the ability to advise and prescribe to those struck by misfortune.

Through all the years of slavery and hardship in Cuba, *babalawos* were at once priests, doctors, and counselors for the poor. If they enjoyed great prestige, it was for the hard work and long hours that they offered for the good of the needy.

Padrino himself "made Ifa," that is, mastered the knowledge and received the fundamental tools of Ifa in 1944 in Havana.[1] He was initiated by Quintin Lecon, one of the most respected *babalawos* on the island. When he came to New York in 1946, he was the only *babalawo* in the city. None who have come since have even approached his prestige and command of the tradition.

Those who come to consult Padrino see not only this history but a source of eternal wisdom, a divine language instituted by Olodumare himself. In Ifa, they seek spiritual help in meeting the ordinary problems of life: help with health, money, love. They seek a knowledge of destiny, of the will of Olodumare as it touches their pursuit of happiness.[2]

Padrino keeps this tradition alive in his consulting room in the Bronx. At his table, amid the splendor of his private shrine, he may "read Ifa" for as many as one hundred people a week. On most days, a few querents can be found waiting patiently downstairs as he sees each in turn for fifteen or twenty minutes. Today I too am waiting to see him. I have come to see Ifa at work and perhaps to listen to its ancient wisdom.

Six or seven people are sitting around the basement room; a television is on low, but no one is watching. Madrina is sitting with us, stringing yet another ritual necklace and chatting with the different callers. Two small children drift in and out looking for distractions. An old *santera* in a white cotton dress and headkerchief turns to me and asks if it is my first time consulting Padrino. "He is the real thing," she tells me. "The first time that Padrino read for me, he told me the story of my life. He knew all the things that had ever happened to me and all the things that ever would happen. You'll see."

A younger woman hears us and can not resist her own testimonial. She first came to Padrino three years ago. He read Ifa and asked her if she had pains in her abdomen. She was startled and a little scared, for she had. He began to ask her intimate questions about her menstrual cycles. Now she was scared and suspicious. "You have an ovarian cyst," he told her. She should see a doctor at once, take special herbal baths, and make a special sacrifice to Oshun. The doctor, of course, found the cyst and treated it, but Ifa and Oshun completed the cure with herbs.

The older *santera* has been nodding her head in agreement, and both women say, almost at the same time, "It is a happy religion, a beautiful religion."

Padrino calls me, and I go up the stairs and into his room. It is just as splendid as I remember it: banks of fresh flowers and food offerings before seemingly hundreds of statues of the saints and emblems of the *orishas*. Padrino is seated at the small table to the right of the shrine and invites me to the small stool opposite him. He is a bit tired but gracious. "Let's see what's what," he says. He asks my name and writes it at the top of a small square of paper from a pad. Peeking into the half-open table drawer, I can see a score of similar sheets covered with names and writing.

First there is the fee, fixed by the *orisha* Orula at $5.25 (five to the fourth power). Padrino instructs me to fold a five dollar bill into a tight square around a quarter and bless myself with the packet as a Catholic would make the sign of the cross. The money has now been consecrated to Orula, and we have made the short passage from ordinary to ritual time.

Then, from the drawer containing the old consultation slips, he takes his fundamental tool of Ifa, a chain called an *opele* or *ekwele*. It would be a familiar sight to most Yoruba: a thin chain some fifty inches long, broken at regular intervals by tortoise shell disks about one-and-a-half inches in diameter.

Padrino cups the *ekwele* in his hands together with the folded fee and touches them to my forehead, shoulders, hands, and knees. He sets the bill down, pinches the chain at its center, and lays it on the table. The pieces of shell are delicately curved so that, as they rest on the table, they must fall with either concave or convex side uppermost. Like the more complex process of manipulating palm nuts, the number of possible combinations is two to the eighth power, or 256. As the chain falls, Padrino writes the combinations from right to left on the square of paper. The vertical lines indicate that the concave side of the shell has fallen uppermost, the circles that the convex side has. The figure looks something like this:

```
I    I
I    I
O    I
O    O
```

He then takes from the same drawer in the table a small shell, a stone, and a piece of bone. He begins a series of operations that become very difficult to follow. He asks me alternately to pick up one or two of the objects, to place them in my closed fists, and to conceal from him which hand contains the bone, shell, stone, or nothing at all. He then throws the chain, which directs him to ask me to present either my right hand or my left. This process occurs some seven or eight times.

I cannot help asking Padrino what is going on. He says, "The chain tells me your basic *letra*, your letter." I ask if that is like an *odu*. "Ah, good, you've been reading about the Yoruba people," he says. "Yes, *letra* is the Spanish for *odu*. The shell and bone and stone let me ask Ifa questions for you about the *letra* and he answers me yes or no."[3]

I learn later that the process is called *ire/osugbo*, or "good and bad." It is used by *babalawos* to speak back to the oracle and ask more specific questions of it. If the *odu* warns of danger, for example, the *babalawo* can determine what kind of danger by means of *ire/osugbo*. He would ask the oracle a question requiring a yes or a no, a good or bad answer symbolized by the shell, stone, or bone. When he throws the chain, the "heads/tails" fall of the disks directs him to choose the right or left hand of the querent.

Padrino continues to throw the chain and marks down two more *odus*, right to left:[4]

O	I	I	I	I	I
I	I	O	O	I	I
O	I	I	O	O	I
I	I	I	I	O	O

At last he pauses, looks thoughtfully at the chain, and says, "It's OK."

My troubles, he says, are not caused by anyone else. They are from God. No one wishes me ill; no one has used spiritual forces to cross my path. What I suffer is part of my destiny. Have I had trouble with my head? Headache? Nervousness? Do I have problems with my stomach? Is my father alive? Is he in good health?

From these diagnostic questions, I begin to learn how Ifa divination works. First, it spots the source of troubles and identifies their cause. It reveals the presence of psychic forces and the evil intent that people harbor against each other—what some call witchcraft. *Santeros* believe that, unless these evil intentions are identified and released, they will have physical effects, both on the person who has the thoughts and on their object. Ifa will frequently counsel confession and reconciliation of these thoughts as well as prescribe medicines against them.

But Ifa also demonstrates that not all problems are attributable to the malice of others. Some are connected with one's own destiny, one's *ori* or subconscious personality given by God. Disturbances, imbalances of the *ori*, are problems of the "head" and, thus, are manifested in headaches and nervousness.

In addition to the individual, Ifa also treats the family. One's *ori* is also inherited; it is our genetic disposition "from God." If it is disturbed, one's relationship with one's father may also be. Ifa will frequently prescribe that family members sacrifice together.

An upset stomach is connected to a confused head. "You don't know why you're here," Padrino tells me. I am only dimly aware of the spiritual world around me. "You are a blind man," he says. "You must become skeptical. Observant. You must listen to your head." An upset stomach means that Oshun, the *orisha* of abdominal organs, is speaking to me. "She is behind you. Pray to her. Ask her for things. Thank her. She is calling you."

Padrino tells me to build a little altar to Oshun when I return home. I am to buy a small lithograph of her Catholic image as La Virgin de la Caridad and set before it five yellow candles and five yellow capuccino pastries. Be sure the pastries have sweet sprinkles since Oshun loves sweet words and foods. After five days, I must take the cakes to the river and offer them to the goddess in her natural guise of flowing fresh water. My stomach will calm, my confusion clear, and I will begin to see with new eyes the *orishas* at work in my life. "You'll see, everything will become easier."

"Do you have any questions?" Padrino asks.

I have too many. I ask how he knows that Ifa works.

"Because I have seen it work. Ifa never lies. I ask it every morning how I should spend my day and Ifa advises me. It tells me special things: don't cross water; don't handle money; don't read Ifa again that day. Every time that I have ignored Ifa's advice, I've been sorry. I've been a *babalawo* for nearly forty years and Ifa has never been wrong."

I ask if there are other *babalawos* in New York.

"There are some.[5] I am their *oluwo*, the lord, the senior *babalawo* in the country. Every year we get together to find the *odu* for the whole country for the year and which *orisha* will be strongest in the world for that year. For years the Spanish newspaper *El Diario* has reported our reading and now the *Daily News* is picking it up. This year's *orishas* are Shango and Babaluaye. It's going to be a hard year, struggle and sickness."

I notice against the wall, behind Padrino's chair, a round wooden tray some two feet in diameter. The tray surface itself is recessed about one quarter of an inch into the wood, leaving a rim about an inch wide. Carved at the four cardinal points on the rim are four almond-eyed faces. "Yes," says Padrino, "the tray is called an *okpon.*" He received it during his initiation in Havana. The four faces are of Eleggua, the mischievous trickster, who must be appeased if the correct interpretation of Ifa's message is to come through. His carved face reminds the *babalawo* that the spirit of chance and disorder pervades every attempt to learn the divine order of Olodumare.

I ask when the board is used.

"On special occasions. When we really have to get deep." The *ekweke* chain is adequate for everyday readings, but certain occasions require the more advanced, laborious, "deep" method of palm nuts, *yefa* dust, and *okpon* tray.

"I'll use the palm nuts when you're ready to receive the hand of Orula, an initiation when you are halfway on the road to being a *babalawo* yourself. Then we'll find out what your path is in Ifa. For now it is Oshun behind you on your road *en santo,* on the way of the *orishas.* Listen for her."

Time is getting on, and Padrino asks if there is anything else I want to know. I want to know everything. Would he conclude by telling me a *pataki,* a story about Ifa?[6]

"Now remember," he says, "you can't know everything. And I can't tell you everything. It takes time. You have to have patience to learn about the *orishas.* And you have to listen. Do you understand?" He tells this story.

Once, back in the beginning, at holy Ile-Ife, Orunmila was the greatest *babalawo* in the land. He read Ifa for commoner and king alike and always told the truth. If the oracle spoke of misfortune, Orunmila would say so. If it identified dishonesty, he would reveal it.

This lack of guile was not always appreciated by his clients. More than once, the vanity of a powerful man was pricked, and Orunmila found himself beaten and exiled with only his Ifa tools and trusted dog for comfort.

So he and the dog would travel to the next town and begin over again. Despite all dangers, Orunmila's dog was always loyal to him. Through thick and thin, the dog stayed with the *babalawo* and strove to be like him in every way, honest and upright.

One day, Orunmila read Ifa for the king of Ede, a pompous tyrant. The oracle told the king that he had seized the throne unjustly and was hoarding the wealth of the city for himself. The king was furious with Orunmila for this message and sent him away in a rage. Fuming alone in his palace that night, the king decided that he would teach the *babalawo* a lesson in manners, and he sent his soldiers to Orunmila's house to deliver a royal beating.

When the soldiers arrived at Orunmila's door, he ran and hid in the closet. The soldiers asked the dog where his master was for they had a special gift for him from the king.

Cheerfully, the dog ran to the closet. "Come out, come out Orunmila," he barked. The soldiers hauled poor Orunmila out of the closet and gave him the beating of his life.

That night, when Orunmila hobbled out of town, all he carried were his Ifa tools and a cat.

Padrino can see that I am puzzled by the story.

"Think about it," he says. "You must learn more about the religion. Come back soon and I will take you further on the road. You are going to need your warriors, *orishas* to protect you."

It was not until much later that I thought about Padrino's purpose in telling me the story, and I realized just who was Ifa and who was his faithful but naive little dog.

6

WARRIORS

When I next return to the Bronx, Padrino is glad to see me. I prostrate myself before the *orisha* within him, palms flat on the floor. He gives me his blessing, and the ritual embrace is warm and genuine. "You look great," he says. "Your good fortune is like a tree. I have planted the seeds and I see that it is growing."[1]

He explains that he has taken the first step in opening up my path of growth *en santo*, in saintliness, in the way of the *orishas*. He has made for me the fundamental symbols of the warrior *orishas*, Eleggua, Ogun, and Oshosi. He has also prepared for me the symbols of the *babalawo*'s protection: a beaded necklace and bracelet as well as the staff of the herbalist, the *osun*. These, he assures me, have been prepared especially for me as Ifa has directed. When I receive them, I will be his godchild, armed with the aggressive force of the warrior *orishas* and protected by the herbal power of the *babalawo*.[2]

The costs of materials, the time spent on their preparation and consecration, must be reflected with an equal commitment on my part. There is a *derecho*, a fee. I remember Padrino's reputation as a "businessman," and I wonder just how "observant," how "skeptical" I should be. Yet it is the way of the *orishas* that one must give in order to receive. It is clear that I must give something of myself in order to enter this world. It may as well be money. The fee is a sacrifice, but not an onerous one. It will be well spent. I plunge.

We climb the narrow stairs to Padrino's private shrine. The huge plaster Christ still presides over the hundreds of *orisha* objects while fresh fruits and sweets have been placed before each of the shrines. Padrino calls his grandson Marty to witness the ceremonies and practice his Lucumi. "I made Oshun when I was only seven," says Marty, who is now eleven. "I'm studying with Viejo to be a *babalawo*. I'm already half way there, aren't I grandpa?"

"We'll see," says a skeptical Padrino.

Marty spreads a reed mat before the *canastillero,* the large wooden armoire that now holds the stones of Padrino's *orishas.* I kneel on the mat, hands on the floor, and repeat after Padrino the Lucumi greeting to Ifa: *iboru iboya ibochiche,* "may Ifa accept the sacrifice." Marty places the fundamental symbols of the warrior *orishas* before me—the concrete bust of Eleggua, Ogun's cauldron of tools, Oshosi's iron bow and arrow. Next to these he adds the bird staff of Osun and a beaded necklace and bracelet.

Padrino begins to instruct me in the significance and care of each. "Eleggua is your first *orisha.* He is the lord of the *caminos,* the opener of the ways. Be sure to always respect him. When you offer something to an *orisha* or an ancestor always offer a part of it to Eleggua. All the *orishas* must share with Eleggua. They can't help you without his permission."

My Eleggua appears much like the ones in the *botánica*: a three-inch cone of grey concrete with cowrie shells for eyes and mouth. He has "tribal" scars on his cheeks, and thrusting through the point of the cone is a tiny knife blade, reflecting Eleggua's power as a warrior and cutter of spiritual paths.[3] But this Eleggua is uniquely mine, for Padrino has placed inside it a combination of herbs specially prepared for me.

"If you speak to your Eleggua, Eleggua will speak to you. Every morning you should greet him. Call him with three raps on the floor and three dashes of cold water. Sing:

Tuto omi tuto tuto Laroye Orunla ache.

Cool, fresh water cools Laroye Eleggua, the *ashe* of Ifa.

"This is your first lesson *en santo*, in the way of the saints. If you learn to speak, you may learn to listen. Eleggua will speak to you in your life. Pay attention to your luck. That's the voice of Eleggua."

But I can influence my luck. Eleggua is a hungry *orisha*. I can offer him food. Padrino tells me that I should offer Eleggua toasted corn and yams. I can give him tobacco and rum to keep him keen and happy. Tobacco smoke can be blown on his concrete head, while rum should be sprayed from my mouth to his. When serious help is needed, I must offer him something stronger still, sacrifices of his favorite animals—roosters, smoked fish, smoked possum, and goat. The blood of some of these foods is poured on his image and fortifies him to open up my luck. Eleggua will move heaven and earth if I am generous, sincere—and lucky. He is not the most responsible of *orishas*. While he works quickly and with great force, he is sometimes like a little child who can be sent on an errand but will not always go.

"If your warriors need to eat these foods you must bring them here and we will feed them together," Padrino says. "You are not ready yet to offer these animals yourself. You need a higher initiation which will come when you have learned the lessons of this one."

Next Marty places before me the cauldron of Ogun with its iron tools. It too is like the *botánica* version, but the tools are clearly handmade at Padrino's basement forge.

"Ogun walks with Eleggua. He is there for you too. He's a warrior and he'll fight for you if you ask him. Ogun will usually eat what Eleggua eats though sometimes you must come to me to find out what he wants. You will see that we will only feed him male animals because he needs his strength."

Padrino does not reveal what several *santeros* later tell me: that Ogun's tools can be used in very aggressive symbolic ways to harm others. Of course, these *santeros* assured me, they themselves would never do such a thing; still, one must know how it is done to protect oneself.

Padrino continues patiently the elementary explanations that he has given so many times before.

"The bow and arrow are those of Oshosi, the hunter of Ketu. He will protect you outside your home. He will keep you from trouble with the law. Oshosi also hunts with Eleggua and Ogun and so he will usually share their food. Put Eleggua, Ogun, and Oshosi at the door of your home. They will keep out any evil that may come in from the outside. Now you have your warriors. Do you have any questions?"

I ask Padrino how I will know what the warriors want and how to satisfy them.

"You must learn to listen to them. Pay attention to your life. What is happening in your life? Are you lucky or unlucky? This is not an accident. This is the *orishas*. But I will teach you a simple way to listen."

Padrino tells me the story of Obi. In the beginning, Obi was an *orisha* living in Ile-Ife, the world's first city at the center of the earth. He was known to be honest and kind and a friend to all. As a reward for his honesty, Olofi, the king of Ile-Ife, placed him high in the palm tree, the sixteen-branched tree of life, symbol of the order of the world. He dressed him in a garment of shining white. But Obi became vain and haughty in these surroundings and began to snub his old friends, particularly Eleggua the trickster.

One day, Obi decided to celebrate a big feast and told Eleggua to invite everyone of importance in Ile-Ife. Eleggua saw his opportunity to test Obi's friendship, and he invited the dirtiest beggars and vagabonds of the city. When Obi arrived to greet his assembled guests and saw only these wretches, he became enraged and threw them all out of his house.

When Olofi the king heard of this mean spiritedness, he decided to teach Obi a lesson. He arrived at Obi's door dressed as a beggar. Obi refused him alms, and Olofi replied, "Obi, see who I am?" Suddenly awakened to his pride, Obi pleaded for forgiveness, but Olofi rendered a stern sentence. From that day onward, Obi's whiteness and purity would be visible only to those who took the trouble to look beneath appearances inside his shell. He would forever fall from his high place in the palm tree to be used by rich and poor alike. However, he

73

would have an important role in bringing human beings health through his fruit and offering them contact with Olofi, their king, through divination with his shell.

Padrino then teaches me how to use the coconut shell for communication with the *orishas*. First, a fresh coconut is drained, and its shell is broken into four small pieces, called *obinus*, roughly two inches square. The *obinus* are placed in a dish of fresh water, and I am to think carefully of a simple yes-or-no question that I wish an *orisha* to answer. Then I must offer a prayer to God, to all the deceased *babalawos* and *santeros*, to my *santería* godfather and godmother, to Biague, the first Obi diviner, and to Obi himself.

The water is then sprayed three times on the ground for Eleggua, whose fickle goodwill is necessary for all communication with the *orishas*. Then the particular saint to be questioned is invoked and offered small shavings of coconut meat, the number corresponding to the sacred number associated with that *orisha*. The *obinus* are cupped in the hands and touched to the forehead, shoulders, hands, knees, and feet. Then they are passed in the sign of the cross and dropped onto the floor from chest level. Like the Obi of Ile-Ife, they fall from on high, and only their white insides reveal the truth.

Depending on whether the white pulp side of the *obinu* or the dark shell side is uppermost, the oracle reveals five possible answers to the questions asked of it. The possibilities are called *letras* (letters) or *caminos* (roads, ways) and are represented in the diagram below adapted from the work on Obi's oracle by Lydia Cabrera.[4]

○ ○ ○ ○	all white	Alafia
○ ○ ○ ●	3 white, 1 dark	Etawe
○ ○ ● ●	2 white, 2 dark	Eyife
○ ● ● ●	1 white, 3 dark	Ocana Sorde
● ● ● ●	all dark	Oyeku

"Obi speaks only these five *letras*," Padrino tells me. "Alafia means 'yes,' but you should throw again to be sure. If you get Alafia or Eyife again it means the best luck. Etawe means 'it's possible.' Throw again for confirmation. If Alafia, Etawe, or Eyife follow, the answer is a definite yes. Eyife is the highest of all the *letras*. It means good luck and definitely 'yes.' You do not have to throw again after this *letra*. Ocana Sorde means 'no' and you should be alert for evil luck. Oyekun is definitely 'no' and when it falls you should touch your chest and say 'olufina' to avert danger. Oyekun probably means that an *egun*, a dead person, is calling you and you should ask again to see what he wants."

"This is the beginning," Padrino says. "You are on the road to be a priest of the religion. Obi is the first step to Ifa and Eleggua is the first *orisha*. You are on the way."

Time is getting on now, and the *osun* staff, necklace, and bracelet still remain. The *osun* is a short six-inch staff topped by a tin rooster, which stands on a small herbal receptacle ringed with small bells.

"These things mean that you are a member of my house. Osun is your life. Place him high, close to God. If Osun falls it is a serious warning to you. It's a message that your life may be in danger. Come quickly to me. I will ask Ifa and he will show us what to do about it. This is how to dance with Osun."

Padrino has me rise and places Eleggua in my left hand and Osun high above my head in my right. He shows me how to dance on my right leg, clockwise ringing my Osun bells.

"Osun is called by the bells. He will protect you now." Padrino then chants in Lucumi while I dance. After several revolutions he has Marty complete the prayer.[5] It seems to me that Marty does pretty well, but Padrino has him repeat it until he has it perfectly.

I return to the mat and am given the final symbols of my entry into Padrino's *ile*. Chanting in Lucumi and periodically quizzing Marty, Padrino places on my left wrist the beaded bracelet (*ide*) and around my neck the necklace (*eleke*). Both are of alternating yellow and green plastic beads strung on cotton thread.[6] The *ide* fits snugly around the wrist; the necklace is looser, some fourteen inches in diameter. "Be careful who you show these to," Padrino cautions. "They have great power but you must always be on guard who knows you have them."

Now Padrino stands me up straight and smiles a warm smile. "I am your godfather, you are my godchild. We will help each other, OK?"

But my initiation is far from complete. As we go downstairs for coffee, Padrino says, "'You must come back next week to balance the warriors with Madrina's *orishas*. The warriors are your strength but you must develop your head. This work must be done by your godmother. Arrange a time with *madrina* to receive her *elekes*.

7

ELEKES

Dutifully, I come back to the *ile* in the Bronx a week later, prepared to receive the *elekes,* the beaded necklaces of the five great *orishas.* Madrina has told me to wear my oldest clothes and to bring with me a new set, entirely white. Once again, I am also to bring the *derecho,* the fee for the *orishas.* It is a substantial one: more than I want to spend, but within my power to raise without borrowing. It will mean no luxuries for a few months—a small commitment.

Several people are in the basement when I arrive. Madrina is once again stringing necklaces and chatting with a young stylish woman in her twenties and two elderly Cuban women both in thin white cotton dresses. The young woman is Maria, Madrina and Padrino's daughter, and she has come over from Queens to assist at my ceremony today. The other womens' names I never learn.

In a corner, Padrino is carrying on an earnest conversation with a short, wiry man in his forties. I make the ritual greeting to Padrino and am introduced to Mr. Gonzales. He is puffing rapidly on a big cigar, and he seems loud and aggressive. He nods to me and quickly turns his attention back to Padrino. I talk with the women, and Madrina serves hot strong coffee, but I cannot help hearing snatches of Padrino and Mr. Gonzales's conversation.

Mr. Gonzales returned to Cuba last year and "made Ifa," that is, received the sacred tools and knowledge of Ifa, the *orisha* of divination and the patron of *babalawos*. He is quite proud that he was initiated in Matanzas, a rural province east of Havana.[1] He wants now to establish himself as a *babalawo* in New York and is seeking Padrino's sponsorship. But he seems unlikely to get it. Padrino is quizzing him on Lucumi songs, but interrupting and correcting him before he can hardly begin them.

"But señior, this is how it is done in Matanzas," pleads Mr. Gonzales.

"It cannot be done that way," says Padrino flatly. "If that is what you have been taught, you have been taught wrong."

Mr. Gonzales puts up weaker and weaker protests as Padrino chants the Lucumi songs correctly. I can hear that, in Padrino's version, the tones of the language are more clearly sounded and the songs are longer and so, presumably, more complete. Finally, Mr. Gonzales leaves, humbled and frustrated. But Padrino is saddened by the encounter. He walks over to me and says, "These newly made *babalawos* are worth nothing. They are taken in by phonies who know nothing and teach nothing. Then they walk around saying, 'Respect me, I'm a *babalawo*.' I tell you the religion is in trouble."

Padrino is going to Manhattan to do some errands. As he leaves he says, "Pay attention to Madrina today. It is the only way to grow properly in the religion."

Soon after Padrino leaves, Madrina begins my instruction. "Today is a good day for you. You will receive the *elekes*. The warriors are a thing from men. Only a *babalawo* can give you warriors. They are hard and will give you strength. The *elekes* will also give you strength but a different kind. They may only come from a woman, your *madrina*. They bring you strength for your head. This is your first step *en santo*, to prepare your head for your *orisha*.

"Padrino says that it is Oshun that I should prepare you for. I, too, am an Oshun. She is a lovely *orisha*. She will help you.

"You know when you have headaches or are confused? It means that you are not paying attention to the *orishas* who talk to you through your head. Your head is your person, your soul. It must be kept cool and clear. So the first thing that we do today will be the *ebori eleda,* washing your head."

The ceremony begins with a *limpieza,* a purification. I am taken to the bathroom and stretched out over the tub. Each of the four women in turn, Madrina, Maria, and the other two *santeras,* wash my head with an herbal preparation called *omiero.* [2] *Omiero* is an infusion of herbs and water made sacred to the *orishas* by special chants and a few drops of the sacrificial blood of their special foods. After each bath in the *omiero,* my head is rinsed from a bucket of river water scooped with a large, decorated shell. As each priestess scrubs, she sings softly in Lucumi. The air is thick with the sweet smell of herbs.

Madrina then instructs me to stand in the running shower, rip off the old clothes that I am wearing, stand firmly on top of them and wash my whole body with the *omiero* and river water. If I were a woman, she says, the *santeras* would rip the clothes themselves, but I would prefer to do it myself, wouldn't I? I am left alone to follow Madrina's instructions.

When I emerge from the herbal shower, I dress in the new, white clothes that I have brought. I return to the basement, and Madrina asks me to kneel beside her. She gently places my head in her lap and slowly combs my hair.

"Your head is clean now," she says quietly. "Your past is no more and your thoughts are cool and clear."

"After the *limpieza* we have the *rogación de la cabeza,* the prayer over the head." She takes me upstairs to Padrino's shrine room, and, as I did last week, I kneel on a reed mat facing the *canastillero,* the armoire that contains the *orisha* stones. She calls for her granddaughter to assist her in this part of the ceremony. A shy little girl not more than five years old enters and stays close to her grandmother. "This is Lydia, Maria's daughter. She's a priestess too. She made Oya when she was only three. We'll see if she remembers her prayers today. It's difficult to get her to pay attention."

Madrina begins a long chant in Lucumi and the little girl pretends to keep up. It sounds like a litany with the names of *orishas* and people interspersed.

"'This is the *moyuba*. When you greet the *orishas* you must begin with God, Olodumare, then the *orishas* in the order that you receive them, then the line of *santeros* who have brought the teachings down to you, and then the *orishas* of all those present. You can say it in English or Spanish now, later I will teach you the proper Lucumi."[3]

She then anoints cardinal points of my body with a sticky preparation of cocoa butter, grated coconut, and a kind of chalk called *cascarilla* or *efun* made from dried egg whites. My head, throat, wrists, palms, and feet are daubed with white cotton balls, which are left to stick. My head is very tightly wrapped with a large white kerchief. Whiteness, Madrina tells me, is purity. I am beginning to see that the *orishas* respond to whiteness. It is the color of the great *orisha* Obatala, and it is the universal conductor of *ashe*.

"The white things are for health," Madrina says. "Your body is open to evil at those places and the white things will cleanse you of any evil if you step on something or touch something.

"Your head has been cleansed with the *omiero* and river water of Oshun. We will ask her if there is anything else that your head needs."

From a dish on the floor she takes the four small squares of coconut shell—the *obinus*—recites the *moyuba* prayer, and asks Oshun if the *rogación* was done properly. The *obinus* fall with one white and three dark. "What did Oshun say, Lydia?" tests Madrina. "Ocana Sorde, no," replies the little girl. Madrina consults the *orisha* further. Did Oshun want honey applied to the points? Four whites fall. "Alafia," says Lydia. Madrina adds honey to the preparation and asks if everything is alright now. Two whites and two darks appear. "Eyife," chimes Lydia. Oshun is satisfied.

Madrina now walks behind me and asks if the dead who have been invoked to witness the ceremony approve of the way it has been carried out. The shells fall one white and three dark, Ocana Sorde, no. Do they want a candle lit for them? Two whites, two darks, Eyife. Definitely yes. A candle is lit. Is everything all right now? Two whites, two darks, Eyife, definitely yes. "*Orishas* before you, the *eguns*, the dead, behind," Madrina says mysteriously.

"Now is the time for you to ask Oshun for what you want. Your head is clear to listen to her. Sit here, be with the *orishas*, and listen to your head. I'll be back in a while." She and her granddaughter leave, and it becomes quiet indeed.

Outside it is twilight, and only the strained light of the New York streets filters through the windows. The small candle behind me throws unsteady light on the world of objects in Padrino's shrine—the giant statue of Christ, the beaded *oshes* of Shango, the scores of food offerings. I am scrubbed and dressed in stiff new white clothes. My head is wrapped, and everything smells of coconut and honey. I am called to be still, to listen to the immense power of the silence.

Sometime later, Madrina returns with her daughter, little granddaughter, and one of the *santeras* who washed my head and who is now introduced to me only as "a daughter of Yemaya." "We are all priestesses," Madrina says, "even this little one. It is time for us to give you your *elekes.*"

I continue to kneel on the mat. Madrina stands before me while Maria is on my right, the old *santera* on my left, and Lydia behind me. Madrina again recites the *moyuba* and holds before me a necklace of small plastic beads, strung singly on a cotton thread some fourteen inches in diameter. The color pattern alternates between three black beads and three red ones, the sacred number and colors of Eleggua.

"This is the *eleke* of Eleggua, the opener of the ways, the master of the roads. He will open your path for you. He will bring you health, luck, tranquillity, and all the good things of life."

She drops the necklace to the ground before me, instructs me to pick it up, kiss it, and return it to her. Then all four priestesses gingerly place the necklace over my wrapped head, singing a short song to Eleggua.

The second necklace Madrina drops before me is white with clear beads interspersed. The pattern is more complex, and it is only later that I see that it is symmetrical, working both ways out from one large clear bead to a large white one, then four clears, four whites, four clears and twenty-four whites.

"This is the *eleke* of Obatala. He is the great *orisha* of the religion, like God himself. All the *orishas* respect Obatala and you must also. He is pure and wise. He will bring you health, luck, tranquillity, and all the good things in life."

Again the *eleke* is dropped, picked up, kissed, and placed over my head, clinking atop the one of Eleggua.

The third necklace is blue and clear with large red beads at regular intervals. Later I see that it is symmetrical beginning with a large red bead, then three blues, three clears, three blues, then seven clears, seven blues, and seven clears, telescoping back to the large red bead.

"This is the *eleke* of Yemaya, the mother of the waters, the owner of the sea. She makes everything clean. She will bring you health, luck, tranquillity, and all the good things in life."

The fourth necklace is simply strung with alternating red and white beads.

"This is the *eleke* of Shango. He is the owner of thunder and strength. He will protect you in battle. He will bring you health, luck, tranquillity, and all the good things in life."

The last necklace is strung almost entirely with gold beads, alternating twenty-five gold, a red, a clear, and a red, then returning to twenty-five gold beads.

"This is the *eleke* of your mother Oshun. She is the owner of sweet things, of love and gold, of money and things of the heart. She will bring you health, luck, tranquillity, and all the good things in life."

The last *eleke* is set in place, and all is quiet for a moment. The candle flickers.

"What you are feeling now . . . that is the *orishas*. Trust them. They will support you."

Another moment passes.

"You must take care of the *elekes*. Respect them for they have *ashe*. Each pattern is a special *camino*, a special road or path of the *orisha*. In time I will teach you prayers to the *orishas* and you will learn to greet your *orishas* by their special *camino*.[4] For instance, Eleggua has twenty-one different *caminos*. The *elekes* have been soaked in *omiero* and their colors and patterns are the *ashe* of the five great *orishas* of the religion. Wear them always, but be careful who you let know that you have them. Be sure to take them off if you have sex. If one breaks don't try to repair it yourself. Bring it back to me and I will fix it because the proper prayers must be said. A broken *eleke* means a problem with the *orisha* and so I can help you know what to do."

Madrina then shows me how to greet each of the *santeras* present in the manner of a son of Oshun. I lie prone before each of them, switching to alternate sides of my body, touching alternate elbows to the ground.

"That is the *moforoibale*," she says. "It means 'I bow before you.' "

She raises me to my feet and offers the ritual embrace, touching shoulders alternately. "Is your mother still living?" she asks. Yes. "Well, you know the love you have for your family and the love your mother has for you? You are now part of my family, my *ile*, my spiritual family, and we love each other in the same way.[5] Welcome to my family."

8

ASIENTO

The morning is gray and cold when I meet the *iyawo*. Padrino's grandson Marty meets me at the door and leads me down to the basement shrine. It is warm here, and there is a thick smell of good cooking. The light is dim, candles flicker, and several people are sitting quietly looking toward the large niche at the end of the room. There amid bright satin hangings sits a young woman in ritual gown. She is crowned with a high white miter, and her dress has layers and layers of white satin. Across her shoulders are several enormous beaded sashes made of hundreds of intertwined strands. Her hands are crossed at her chest like an Egyptian pharaoh. In one hand is a small cane, completely encrusted with white beads: in the other, a white horsetail switch, the royal *iruke*. The white, royal calm of the entire scene says that the woman is a daughter of Obatala, the king of purity and peace. She is being initiated as a priestess of Obatala's mysteries, and this is her day in state.

As I have been taught, I approach the throne and prostrate before her, *moforoibale*, rolling on my hips and touching alternate elbows to the ground. "Ah," cluck the old *santeras* in attendance, "a son of Oshun." I greet Madrina, an elderly woman introduced as Awolowo, and a young black American woman introduced as Barbara.

I sit quietly by the throne with them, and everyone smiles at each other for some time in the quiet. Awolowo speaks to

84

the royal presence, who replies softly, and all is quiet again. I ask Awolowo if it is permissible for me to speak to the *iyawo*. She nods. I turn to the throne and am greeted with a smile so warm and broad that I am stagestruck. I blurt out that she looks beautiful.

"Well," she replies, "it's my birthday. I have just made Obatala. I am his daughter and I have been born today."

I ask if she feels like a newborn. She laughs and says, "Yes, in a way." She turns to Awolowo. "May I tell him?" Getting a nod, the *iyawo* says, "I have been here in the *ile* lying on the ground for the last five days. I was not allowed to walk or talk and my *yubona*, my sponsor in this initiation, Awolowo, fed me from a spoon like a little baby. All this has prepared my head to receive Obatala. I sure feel different."

I notice that beneath her crown her head is shaved and wonder if this is part of the rebirth symbolism too. I ask her why her head is shaved.

"May I tell?" she asks her *yubona*. Awolowo looks to Madrina. "I will tell him," Madrina pronounces.

"You know that the *orishas* are in the stones. Remember when you faced the *canastillero*? You were facing my *orishas* in their stones. You know too that we feed the *orishas* through their stones. Well, we say that the head of a person is a kind of stone. It, too, is the seat of the *orisha*. So our ceremony this week is called *asiento*, the seating of the *orisha* Obatala in the head of this *iyawo*."

"I am crowned with Obatala. He is seated in my head," says the *iyawo*.

So why is her head shaved?

"So her head could receive the *omiero* and blood offered to the stones," says Madrina. "So the *orisha* could be made to sit there. Today the *orisha* has come to sit in her head and in her stones. See?"

For the first time I see a double line of *soperas* on the floor of the satin throne niche. One set is the *iyawo's*, the other her *madrina's*. Out of them stick the spindly legs of sacrificed fowl. In the corner are two cauldrons of Ogun and two busts of Eleggua, each topped by the severed head of a horned goat. The sight is startling and unsettling for me though I know that they were slaughtered cleanly and with devotion and that their meat will be eaten at a huge feast tonight.

"All the *orishas* ate last night and all the *santeros* will eat tonight," says Madrina.

I ask about the different days of the *asiento* ceremony, and the three *santeras*, each interrupting the other, tell me of an eight-day rite of passage.[1]

For five days, the *iyawo* is kept in prenatal isolation, usually at the home of her godmother, preparing her head for the great rebirth of new life. Against these five days of private transformation are three public ones during which the *santería* community witnesses the new birth. The *iyawo* is shown to be a new person before the community, who give praise to the *orisha* for a new vehicle of *ashe*.

The first day of the three great days is called *el día de la coronación*, when the *orisha* is crowned in the *iyawo*'s head. Yesterday was coronation day for this *iyawo*, whose name I later learn is Mercedes. Her head was shaved and marked with sacred signs. It was then "fed" with blood and herbs, sealing it as a seat of the *orishas*. She was then invested with the stones of five great orishas: Yemaya, Oshun, Oya, Shango, and her patron Obatala. The stones, like her head, were bathed and fed. Since Obatala is Mercedes's patron, only white animals were offered. Today the thick smells of cooking that fill the shrine are doves and chickens, mutton and goat, sacred to Obatala.

Last night, too, Mercedes was invested with the tools and emblems of her *orisha*. She received small white-metal tools to "work Obatala," that is, to direct his *ashe* to solve specific problems. She was also presented with Obatala's regal emblems, the cane and horsetail *iruke* that she now carries in state. Across her shoulders were placed the huge *collares de mazo*, giant beaded sashes sacred to each *orisha* and worn over the shoulder on ceremonial occasions. Finally, with the stones she was given *dilogun*, cowrie shells sacred to each *orisha* and used for divination.

The ceremonies of *el día de la coronación* reach their climax when the *iyawo* is ritually crowned, dressed in regal finery appropriate to her *orisha*. She is enthroned on the *pilón*, the sacred mortar stool of Yoruba kings. The stones of each *orisha* are placed over her head, and songs are sung in honor of each. At this moment, the community waits for the patron *orisha* to descend and mount the *iyawo*. The combination of isolation, chants, and ringing instruments leaves the *iyawo* ready to receive the *orisha* in her head.

As the *santeras* are explaining this dramatic moment of illumination to me, I remember the Lydia Cabrera saying that the Lucumi term for *asiento* is *kariocha*, "to put the *orisha* over the head."[2] In the juxtaposition of head and stones, I begin to think that I am getting close to the heart of the santería mysteries. In ceremonies requiring great knowledge and devotion, spiritual power is "seated" in stones and in the "head" of the devotee. At *asiento*, the most essential presence of the *orisha* in the world, its stones, is now within the initiate, in her "head," part of her very soul, her second nature. The mysteries lie in the spiritual power and ceremonial control of one's "head." I remember an old *santera* saying to me once, "Since I became an *asientada* I don't wear the *elekes* any more because the *orishas* are in my head."

I ask the *iyawo*, Mercedes, if she is tired after such a great day. "Oh, no," she replies serenely. "Today is *el día del medio*, the middle day, and everything is easy."

Madrina, Awolowo, and Barbara continue with my instruction. They tell me that the second day of the *asiento* cycle is a day for relaxation and receiving visitors. Mercedes is presented in state as a new daughter of Obatala. She brings to the community the dignity of a great king, and everyone is brought back to the peace of the original kingdom of Ile-Ife.

Tonight there will be a feast, and the sacrifices of the coronation ceremony, now bubbling on the stove, will feed hundreds. "All the *santeros* will come tonight," says Madrina.

"All will dance with the drums though it will be very peaceful since Obatala forbids alcohol at his court."

"It is very beautiful," she continues. "It is too bad that you can't come because only *santeros* are permitted and you don't have the saint. When you get the saint then you can come."

I ask how I would "get the saint?"

"You must be initiated like Mercedes. You must become an *iyawo* and have the saint seated in your head. But the saint must call you first. Have you been listening?"

I bring the subject back to *asiento*. The three *santeras* enthusiastically tell me of the third great day of *asiento*, *el día del Ita*. The day focuses on a deep divination or *ita* performed for the *iyawo* by a specialist called an *italero*. The *ita* reveals the basic patterns of the *iyawo*'s new life *en santo*. This life reading illuminates the initiate's path through the troubles and joys that lie ahead. I ask if it is like Ifa.

"Yes and no," answers Barbara. She makes a careful comparison. "Only a *babalawo* can read Ifa and there are 256 *odu* or *letras*. The *ita* is done by an *italero* and there are only sixteen *letras*. In Ifa Orula speaks with the voice of God. With the *ita* the *orishas* speak directly. Orula speaks with nuts or the *ekwele* chain. The *orishas* speak through shells. We call the shells *dilogun*, which means sixteen. Sixteen is a sacred number in the religion."[3]

Madrina tells a story of *dilogun*. In the beginning at Ile-Ife, Orula the diviner was married to Yemaya, the mother of the *orishas*. He used both Ifa and *dilogun* at the time, and he was in much demand throughout the kingdom. What he did not know, however, was that Yemaya had secretly learned the art of divination by *dilogun* shells and was receiving querents on her own when he was called away. One day he returned home unexpectedly and caught Yemaya in the process of throwing *letra* twelve, Eyila Che Bora.

"Stop!" cried the enraged Orula. From that day on, the children of Yemaya, that is, all the initiated children of the *orishas*, can use the dilogun shells. But they may not interpret any of the *letras* beyond *letra* twelve. The remaining four are still the special province of the children of Orula, the *babalawos*. "Whenever those *letras* come," Madrina says, "I take the matter to Padrino."

The *iyawo* has been paying careful attention to this discussion, for the day of *ita* is still to come. She asks Awolowo, her *yubona*, "What will happen?"

"The *italero* will tell you your future," says Awolowo. "It will be very beautiful. You will learn how to avoid sicknesses, how to get money and keep your husband happy. You will learn who are your friends and who are your enemies. You will learn what are your lucky and unlucky days and what foods are good and bad for you. You will learn how to ask the *orishas* for help in ways that they can't refuse. You will learn your whole life."

We have been talking for nearly an hour, and several people have come to prostrate themselves before the *iyawo* and the senior priestesses. Some have listened to our discussion, while others have started quiet conversations among themselves. A large woman wearing a big red hat and laden with gold jewelry joins us. "The *iyawo* is the bride of the *orisha*," she asserts severely. "She must obey him in every way." A smile begins to show on her face. "At least for a year."

Everyone around laughs, some a little shyly. Madrina explains that, for a year after *asiento*, the new bride must abstain from all sexual activity. "Only the *orisha* is her husband."

Another door is opening on the *orishas'* mystery. I am struck by the idea that not only are the *orishas* our elders and rulers but they can also be our lovers. The relationship between human and *orisha* can be seen as a sexual one, a mystical union in which the *orishas* are "inside" their brides. They "descend" and "mount" their devotees.

"It doesn't matter if the *iyawo* is a man or a woman," Madrina says. "We call them both *iyawo*."

And what if both the *orisha* and the *iyawo* are the same sex?

"The *orishas* have many *caminos*, many roads. They can be either men or women."

The big woman in red and gold puts in seriously, "It's not only sex that a bride must give her husband." She and the other priestesses tell me of the *ewos*, the restrictions or guidelines that the *iyawo* must follow during her one-year novitiate. Besides sexual continence, the *iyawo* must always dress in white and keep her head covered. She is forbidden to visit bars, jails, cemeteries, hospitals, and other places of possible contamination. She is forbidden alcohol, profane language, shaking hands, and eating with a knife and fork. Among the other members of the *ile*, the *iyawo* cannot accept money for assisting at ceremonies.[4]

All these *ewos* reinforce the betwixt-and-between status of the newborn *santera*. They bring home to her the depth of the change her life has undergone and the commitment necessary to live a life *en santo*. The *ewos* also demonstrate that the life of the *orishas* hearkens back to the natural life of Ile-Ife. They develop a critical awareness that Western customs such as hand shaking and tableware are not those of the African Eden.

Perhaps the most important *ewos* of all are the lifelong food restrictions that the *iyawo* assumes. From *asiento* onward, she will eat only the food acceptable to her patron *orisha*, and she must avoid those forbidden by the spirit. For Mercedes, the new bride of Obatala, this will mean a lifelong abstention from alcohol.

I ask Awolowo about this, and she tells me that, back in Ile-Ife, Olodumare had commissioned the sculptor Obatala to create the world. He began beautifully, but stopped frequently to refresh himself with palm wine. Before long, he became too drunk to work properly, and the obvious problems with the design of the world are the result. Since then, he has dedicated himself to sobriety and calm responsibility and so forbids his children to make the mistakes he did.

As Awolowo has been telling the story, the still placid *iyawo* has been receiving more visitors, and the room is nearly full of happy people. Madrina has risen to greet the more distinguished guests and supervise the cooking. Efundare, the old Puerto Rican spiritualist, is here, and so is Olatutu, the shy black American Egyptologist. Padrino has arrived, and his godchildren are lining up before him for their prostrations. I know that it is getting to be time to go. I ask the *iyawo* for her blessing, thank Awolowo and Barbara for their patient explanations, and take my leave.

I am last in the line of Padrino's greeters, and he has a moment to chat. I remark on the beauty of the *iyawo*'s throne. Padrino is somewhat rueful. "Yes, it's beautiful," he says, "but it is no substitute for knowing the ceremonies. Too many *santeros* made in America think that if they spend a lot of money then the saint will be made well. In Cuba *asiento* wasn't very expensive but in the old days it would take nine months to make a saint. I guess we can't do that anymore, but you knew then that the head was really prepared. It's so expensive now. The animals alone can cost one thousand dollars."

I ask him how much an *asiento* in America should cost.

"It depends on the saint. Each *orisha* wants different animals and fruits, different clothes, different dances. I suppose anywhere from twenty-five hundred to five thousand dollars. Some crooks charge ten thousand dollars and do it completely wrong. They improvise everything and cheat you. Take your time and learn about the religion before you commit yourself."

Madrina interrupts us to say to me that the drummers are arriving and all non-*santeros* must leave. "You have learned a lot today," she says, "but you are not ready to learn everything."

She moves on, and Padrino says quietly, "Madrina is very strict and she is right to be so. But you can come to a *bembe* we're going to be having in a couple of weeks. One of my godchildren is celebrating her fifth birthday *en santo* and everyone is invited. The *bembe* is a party for the *orishas* with drums. You can be my guest. No one will object."

9

BEMBE

It is a crisp and cold Saturday afternoon when I find my way through the Bronx tenements to Padrino's *bembe*. From some way off, I can see that many people are coming, and several are bunched at the door as they are being admitted to the basement shrine. All faces are friendly and expectant. Quick ritual greetings are exchanged as people hustle through the door to get in from the cold.

Inside, the room is filled with milling people. Coats are stacked in the corners, and conversations fly in Spanish and English. The niche that two weeks ago enshrined the *iyawo* Mercedes is now curtained off with a high white cloth. The sound of rattles and Lucumi chants can be heard from the other side.

I see Maria, Padrino and Madrina's daughter from Queens who assisted in giving me the *elekes*. I greet her and ask about the music from the sanctuary.

"That's the *oriate*," she says. "He's a special priest who knows all the *suyeres*, the Lucumi prayers. He's preparing Olade's *fundamentos* for her *cumpleaños*, her birthday *en santo*."[1]

From time to time, a few voices from behind the curtain respond to the called prayers of the *oriate*, and others outside, especially the older people, also join in. In a while, several people emerge from the sanctuary—a short fair-skinned man in his forties whom I take to be the *oriate*, then Padrino and Madrina and two other women. The women wear white kerchiefs, the men soft brimless caps. One of the women is our hostess, Olade. She is tall, dark, and dressed in a magnificent red gown. Though Padrino had been generous to lend her his house for her festival, all the expenses of entertaining at least one hundred people are hers. She mills around greeting the guests. Several prostrate before her, and she gives them the blessing of Shango, her patron *orisha*.

Madrina and Padrino are also receiving greeting, and I make my way up to them and offer *moforoibale* to each in turn. After his blessing, Padrino says, "Man, we've got a crowd today. I hope the *orishas* come down. You never know. It'll be good for you to meet them."

As we are speaking, three young men thread their way through the crowd carrying large cases that can contain only drums. They have been commissioned by Olade to play for her Shango's rebirthday. The drums will praise Shango and the other *orishas* and the "heads" of important guests. They will also call the *orishas* to descend and join the fiesta.

The drummers greet Padrino, and he introduces me to Ayanwunmi, the leader of the trio. I ask him about the drum he is unpacking.

"This is a *bata* drum.[2] The foundation of the *bata* is a spirit called Aña. That's the basis of the drum's *ashe*. These drums here have been consecrated, but they aren't really fundamental. Those ceremonies can only be done in Cuba. These drums can call the *orishas* to fiestas, but for the really deep work you still have to go to Cuba."

He begins tuning a drum about two-and-a-half feet long shaped like an hourglass with a goatskin head at each end. One head is quite small, only a few inches across, while the other is considerably larger, well over a foot in diameter. Both heads are ringed by leather belts hung with little bells.

"This one's called the *iya*, the mother drum. It calls the changes for the others. The middle-sized one that Roberto is tuning is called the *itotele* and the little one is the *okonkolo*. They lay down the basic rhythms while the Mother does the talking."

Ayanwunmi is busy, so I thank him and move to the outer edge of the crowd. Maria, Padrino's daughter, is there, and I stand next to her. As we chat, the random beats of tuning subside, and the room becomes hushed.

The three *bata* drummers are seated, drums across their knees facing the sealed shrine. The ceremony begins with a sharp slap of the *iya* followed by the high cracks of the *itotele* and the *okonkolo*. The rhythms are forceful and complex. The high pitches are penetrating.[3]

"They are asking Eleggua to open the way for us," Maria tells me. "If you don't ask Eleggua first he may become insulted and he won't open up the gate for the rest of the *orishas*."[4]

After a few minutes, Eleggua's rhythms give way to another. "Ogun, the hunter," says Maria.

In turn, each of the *orishas* is saluted until the aggressive rhythms of the fiesta's patron, Shango, signal that the opening praises are complete.

As the echos subside, the *ile*, the congregation, reorients itself around the drums, clearing a small area before them for dancing. "Now the party begins," says Maria.

The *oriate* who had been preparing the shrine earlier makes his way to a place beside the drums. He picks up a gourd rattle, the *achere*, and begins to sound a basic rhythm. He begins to sing in a high, nasal voice:

> *Ibarago moyuba*
> *Ibarago moyuba*
> *Ibarago moyuba Elegba Eshulona*
>
> O great one, I salute you
> O great one, I salute you
> O great one, I salute Eleggua, Eshu on the
>   road.[5]

The *ile* responds to the call by repeating the verse, and then drums fall in. The rhythms are more sustained now, and the responses of the people to the singer become increasingly clearer and more forceful. Nearly everyone is swaying to the music and joining in the responses.

Ago ago
Ago ago
Ago ile ago

Open up, open up
Open up, open up
Open up, *ile,* open up.

"Eleggua is loosening everybody up, letting the *ashe* flow," Maria tells me as she dances. After several minutes, a few people come up to the small cleared area and dance before the drums. One old woman moves with particular confidence and energy, and the others encourage her with strong singing and dancing of their own.

"That's Eshubiyi," Maria says a little breathlessly. "She made Eleggua in Cuba years ago. The drums are praising her Eleggua and she's showing her respect."

Eshubiyi dances over to Ayanwunmi and fixes a ten-dollar bill to his sweat-beaded forehead. The *iya* drum ends the rhythm in a flourish, and all applaud.

But the drums' rest is only momentary. Another rhythm starts up, and new dancers come to the fore as their *orisha* is being called.[6] The soloist keeps the basic rhythms with his *achere,* and the *ile* responds to his *orisha* praises more strongly than ever:

Ile gbogbo l'Ogun wa
Ogun wa n'ile
Ogun wa l'ona
Ile gbogbo l'Ogun wa

Ogun is in all houses
Ogun is at home

95

Ogun is on the road
Ogun is everywhere.

The dances show the *orishas* at their best, in motion. The movements mime their personalities. Ogun the hunter slashes his way through the forest. His companion Ochosi draws his bow. Yemaya recalls the rolling of water in motion. She is called to receive her offerings:[7]

> *L'ari oke, l'ari oke*
> *Oke oke Yemaya l'odo*
> *L'ari oke*
>
> Raise your head, raise your head
> Up, Up, Yemaya in the water
> Raise your head

Although all the songs are propelled by the aggressive high cracks of the *bata* drums, each has a different texture, a different spiritual quality of movement.[8]

Eleggua has done his work well, and the rhythms are very strong now. They sustain everyone in the room. All are moving. The music seems to be coming from inside the people as if by their movement they are liberating the sound from within themselves. One woman in particular is carried by this energy, and others begin to channel theirs toward her. The dancing circle clears for her alone, and the drums focus directly on her.

Her eyes are closed, and she is whirling and whirling. She bumps up against the human ring that encloses her and gently rebounds back to the circle's center. The call and response between soloist and congregation has become tighter and more intense. For each praise name of Oshun, the *ile* immediately responds *esho*, "hold": hold the rhythm, hold the *orisha*, hold the whirling dancer. Then, with a sharp slap from the *iya*, she falls to the ground. The drums are silent, and the room echos.

Three *santeras* help her up and begin to escort her from the room. As she parts the crowd, she is clearly a different person. Her eyes are open now and gigantic, their focus open to the whole world. Her face is illuminated with an enormous smile, and she moves her shoulders and hips with sensuous confidence. Oshun has arrived.[9]

The drummers rest, and everyone talks excitedly. "They are preparing her for us," Maria says. "She wants to look her best for the fiesta. You should have a gift for her, even some pennies will do."

A few minutes later, the embodied *orisha* returns resplendent in a gold gown. Her hair is long and unbound, and, like a true African, her feet are bare. She shows the same magical smile and unearthly eyes. The drummers begin her praises, and all join a litany of her praise names. She dances her acceptance of these with grace, and even blows kisses to her votaries. Her dance is sensuous and sweet, moving from deep down her spine.

Occasionally, she brings others out to dance with her. None can match her, but each is pleased with the opportunity. She moves among the enthralled *ile*, kissing and laughing. Then I am startled to see that she is making right for me. Before I can react, she is right before me with a gaze that seems both on and through me at the same time. She speaks. "Owo omomi."

"She's asking for money," someone says. I am paralyzed. This is not a human being before me. It feels as though the drums are inside my head. At last I fumble for my wallet, pull out a bill, and place it in the *orisha*'s outstretched hands.

"Modupe omomi, omo Shango," Oshun responds. She peals with laughter and kisses me hard on the mouth. I am not sure if I am conscious or not at this point.

The *orisha* moves on, and people are smiling at me, swaying to the music. Oshun dances up to the drums and places my bill on Ayanwunmi's forehead. A twenty. He nods, and the *orisha* whispers in his ear. The rhythms begin to change. Maria says, "She called you her child, and child of Shango.[10]

She must have asked the drummers for Shango. After all it's his party."

The rhythms become stronger still. The soloist sings the praises of Shango, and the *ile* responds with one voice. I feel myself lifted, called, carried by the rhythm, alternating between anxiety at the strange sensations and deep calm because the flow is strong and sure. A torrent, but an old and a wise one. As I relax, things seem very slow indeed and crystal clear. I can see every slap of the drummers' hands, notice every nuance of the dancers' shoulders and eyes. People are beginning to look at me and back away. Some seem concerned. I assure them that I am fine, but my voice is rumbling and deep. The words are unfamiliar.

Kawo, Kabiesile. Welcome, Your Majesty. Welcome home.

Maria and Madrina take my arms and bring me through the crowd. It is suddenly hot and close, and I am panting for breath. Maria is pressing my shoulders very hard, and Madrina is blowing and speaking in my ear. I am a bit breathless, but ordinary.

"It's okay," says Maria. "You just got your signals crossed."

"It was a dream," Madrina says softly. "But Shango is speaking to you. Will you listen now?"

When they take me back to rejoin the fiesta, Shango has found a suitable mount. A woman is dancing before the drums in a deep crouch, bringing down each bent leg very hard so that her bare feet slap the basement floor. She is wearing a red and white tunic with rolled-up pants. A red satin sash is tied loosely around her waist. As she turns to face the *ile*, her eyes show the same unearthly gaze, but her face seems a mask of rage. She—or, more properly, he since this body now contains Shango—then begins to dance among the *ile*, his chin thrust out and seemingly haranguing different people. I'm surprised to see that people seem to be speaking back to him in the same tone of voice, a kind of repartee that those who are near enough to hear enjoy. The *orisha* always seems to get the last laugh, however.

As Shango dances and jokes, Oshun enters from the other side of the room. I learn later that she has been in private consultation with several people for whom she had messages.[11] One man she warned to be extra cautious traveling over bridges; for another woman she prescribed herbs for a urinary infection. When Oshun enters, Shango immediately leaves his human devotees and falls before her.

"That woman's Shango is younger than the other woman's Oshun," says Maria, who has been keeping an eye on me. It seems that the sweet *orisha* has cooled some of the rage of the wrathful one, for when Shango rises and they dance together, the energy is calm and composed.

This feels like the heart of the religion at last, a harmony of the human and the divine in dance and joy. The people have brought the *orishas* out of themselves, and now, as one, they are celebrating their link with paradise. They are dancing as they did in Ile-Ife, in the beginning.

One cannot stay in paradise, of course. Everyone is tired, especially the *orishas* who have been dancing, hard, for nearly two hours. Shango has been eating and drinking hard too and is now conducting a last-minute consultation with his hostess, Olade.

The drummers begin the rhythms that will close the fiesta, calling on Eleggua to open the gates and bring the *orishas* back to the invisible world. As if on cue, both mounts fall to the ground and wake up as their former, if exhausted, selves. Olade and Madrina take a pail of water and empty it in the street "to remove any evil," says Maria. The drums sound a final series of praises for the *orishas,* and then all is quiet.

There is food, of course, and gossip and endless comparison between this fiesta and great ones of the past.

"Only two *orishas.* Don't the drummers know the rhythms?"

"Shango told Manuela to stop sleeping around."

"Olade hasn't skimped with the rice and beans."

"The fruit isn't very fresh though."

"Lydia's Oshun is very sweet, very beautiful. But I'm glad Oya didn't come down. These two do not get along at all."

No one mentions my experience, and I begin to wonder if it is in fact a dream.[12] Something was there, something very real indeed, a call to a new reality. It took but a small shift in awareness to see that life is infinitely deeper and more beautiful than most of us ever know. This is the secret of santería, that knowledge and devotion, faith and love, show one what is already there. There is no secret, only God.

PART 3

Santería is a miracle of spirit brought out of crushing human suffering. Its history shows that a people placed under the most difficult conditions imaginable can fashion a spiritual world of beauty and hope. How are we to understand this miracle? How has santería survived, how has it changed, how does it continue to inspire seekers? In this final part, I will try to answer these questions by seeing santería from three interrelated perspectives: as a vital historical link with America's African heritage, as a heroic struggle against racism and poverty, and as a religion of power and grace.

10

ETHNOHISTORY

When Melville Herskovits wrote *The Myth of the Negro Past* in 1941, the myth that he wished to dispel was the widely held notion that black Americans were a people without a past and, thus, without culture or dignity.[1] Herskovits argued forcefully that black Americans could claim a deep and abiding cultural heritage, an "ethnohistory," that the hardships of slave life and the hostility of racial prejudice could not obliterate. In the holds of those dreadful slave ships were men and women carrying with them the skills and wisdom of scores of ancient African civilizations. Though they were scattered and tormented on the plantations of the Americas, they managed to preserve fragments of their cultural past as they prepared to survive in the New World. These cultural fragments Herskovits called "Africanisms," and he documented them in black American arts and agriculture, in folklore and family life, and, most significant, in religion.[2] Herskovits felt that religion was the focus of the African genius, the rock on which Africans would rebuild their sense of themselves in the New World.

In order to understand the reasons why Africanisms were retained or lost in the New World, a process he called acculturation, Herskovits began to compare the African influences on different societies throughout the New World. He personally carried out field work in Haiti, Surinam, Brazil, and Dahomey (Benin). He writes,

From the point of view of the study of Africanisms, also, it is important to know the variation
in Negro customary behavior, traditions, and beliefs over the entire New World as it is to understand the variation in the ancestral cultures
of Africa itself, for only against such a background can the student project a clear picture of
what has resulted from the differing historical
experiences that constitute the essential control
in the research procedure.[3]

When we apply Herskovits's ideas of ethnohistory and
acculturation to santería, we can see that its survival can be
explained by a combination of cultural factors encompassing
its African past and the historical experience of the Yoruba
in Cuba. Following Herskovits, I will speak of three ethnohistorical factors that contributed to the survival of the *orishas*
in Cuba: the Yoruba religious heritage, the social environment
of colonial Cuba, and the influence of the Roman Catholic
church.

If we look at Yoruba religion as the baseline for the
emergence of santería, we can see several features that make
it particularly open to change. One factor that must have
helped Yoruba slaves adapt to the New World was their experience with urbanism. By the time of the slave trade, the
Yoruba had been living in cities for at least one thousand
years.[4] For over two hundred years prior to the terrible slaving
wars of the early nineteenth century, the Yoruba controlled
extensive trade routes throughout the Western Sudan. They
were in constant contact with a wide variety of cultures and
religions, and they were no strangers to pluralism.

Their religious vision was equally cosmopolitan. Their
faith in the spiritual unity of Olodumare and the dynamic
force of *ashe* opened them to a variety of religious viewpoints.
The pantheon of *orishas* continually incorporated new erup-
tions of power from abroad. The dwelling place of the *orishas*
was ultimately *ori*, the head, a spiritual entity capable of cross-
ing the great ocean. The wisdom of this entire tradition could

be epitomized and dispensed from one central source, the memories of the priests of Ifa, the *babalawos*.

This experience with urbanism, pluralism, and theological flexibility gave the Yoruba unique resources for regaining their spiritual equilibrium amid the culture shocks of the New World. Yet we know that Yoruba religion did not survive everywhere in the New World, at least not in easily recognizable forms. If the *orishas* lived on in the United States, they did so under heavy disguises indeed.[5] Why then do we find santería in Havana and not in Charleston?

Herskovits is once again our guide in isolating the social factors that would support or impede the survival of Yoruba religion in the New World. We may begin with the demographic data of colonial Cuba. Fernando Ortiz has shown that, throughout the first two-thirds of the nineteenth century, approximately half the Cuban population was of African descent.[6] The African presence in Cuba must have been strong indeed when we remember that the account of the Epiphany parade cited in chapter 2 shows an easy familiarity with Mandinkas, Araras, and Lucumis.

The American historian of Africa, Philip Curtin, calculates that the majority of slaves brought to the New World in the early nineteenth century were Yoruba and that most of these were headed for Cuba and Brazil.[7] Ortiz speaks of numerous Yoruba *cabildo* associations and of planters' preferences for Yoruba slaves.

The French sociologist Roger Bastide cautions us that the survival of the cultural traits of a particular African people in the New World cannot always be attributed to sheer numbers.[8] If this were so, it would be difficult to explain the continued growth of Fon candombles in Brazil or the Efik societies of Cuba. Still, the influx of such a large number of Yoruba over such a relatively short period of time must be considered a factor in the survival of the way of the *orishas* in Cuba.

Both Herskovits and Bastide point to urbanism as crucial for the survival of African religious institutions in the New World. While the isolation of the countryside might provide a haven for the survival of some Africanisms, life in the cities offered many more opportunities for association and cultural creativity. We have seen that slaves and free people of color dominated many of the trades of colonial Havana, where they often worked as wage laborers loading ships, laundering, carting, and building. Slave life in Havana also offered the greatest opportunity of all—freedom.

Ortiz's nineteenth-century census figures show that free "people of color," *gente de color,* made up approximately one-third to half of Cuba's population of African descent. Herbert Klein argues that this relatively high percentage can be attributed to the institution of *coartación,* the legal process by which a slave could purchase his or her own freedom in a notarized exchange.[9] Though the island enacted a number of restrictive racial laws in the 1840s, this free population continued to provide special economic and cultural opportunities for Africans and people of African descent. The *gente de color* used their economic independence to finance the *cabildos* through which they raised money to buy their enslaved members' freedom and to support the dances and ceremonies of the motherland.

With the majority of Cuba's *gente de color* concentrated in cities, particularly in Havana, Africans had unique resources to preserve the old traditions. Santería owes its origins to the urban slaves and *gente de color* in the heterogeneous, bustling world of Creole Havana. It was there that they seized the opportunities to establish the independent and self-administered *cabildos* that supported ritual life. The urban setting provided the occasions for both the blending and the segmentation of cultures that underlay the emergence of santería.

Reviewing the social factors that gave rise to santería, we can see that a large part of the explanation can be attributed to the ethnohistory of the Yoruba in Cuba. Santería was created by large numbers of Yoruba men and women arriving in Cuba in the time of a single generation, working in Havana and other towns with large populations of free countrymen, and with the hope of freedom themselves.

The final factor in this ethnohistorical explanation for the survival of santería lies in the religious life of the Yoruba's captors. Bastide recognizes the importance of European religions by dividing his discussion of African-derived religions into two contexts, Catholic and Protestant.[10] As the official religion of colonial Cuba, Catholicism is the seedbed for the survival of the *orishas.*

Following Frank Tannenbaum, Herbert Klein argues that the legal institutions of the Catholic New World provided a modicum of rights for the slaves and thus mitigated sufferings they frequently endured in non-Catholic countries.[11] Apologists have used this research to engage in futile and heartless debates about the relative benignity of different slave systems—Latin tolerance versus English coldness, Latin cruelty versus English humanitarianism—stereotypes irrelevant to the conditions of slave life.[12] What Tannenbaum and Klein establish is that the Catholic church did play a decisive role in the lives of the slaves under its influence and was a key factor in the development of santería.

According to Tannenbaum and Klein, the church's authority to enforce the Spanish crown's Laws of the Indies gave it powers over slaves' lives that the established and nonconformist Protestant churches lacked in the English-speaking New World. The Catholic church had the power to protect sacramental slave marriages, which must have contributed to stable slave communities in important ways. Klein attributes the high percentage of free blacks in Cuba to the church's sponsorship of manumission and *coartación.*

Critics charge that, though the church was empowered to protect the rights of slaves, its failure to do so, particularly on the hellish sugar plantations, voids any case for a positive view of church-slave relations.[13]

Stepping back from the moral issue of the failure of religious institutions to practice what they preach, others have criticized Klein for believing that religion, not economics, determined the state of slave society.[14] It is impossible to say what determines social institutions, but Klein provides strong evidence that Catholicism was a crucial factor in the development of santería.

According to Klein, the Catholic church was the motivating force behind the *cabildos,* the associations of slaves from the same African nation. He cites an eighteenth-century bishop, Pedro Augustin Morel de Santa Cruz, who used the *cabildos* as a base for catechizing the slaves. Klein writes,

> When he [Bishop Morel] took up his diocese he found that in the city of Havana there were twenty one Negro clubs or cabildos, each with its own house, where Negroes of both sexes gathered during the holidays and Sundays to drink, dance "in extremely torrid and provocative dances," and commit other excesses too sinful to mention. Many told the bishop that it was better to leave these cabildos alone for they provided a reasonable outlet for the slaves and freedmen without causing undue harm. But he declared: "Not being satisfied with similar scruples, I attempted the gentle method of going by turns to each of the cabildos to administer the sacrament of confirmation, and praying the holy rosary with those of that organization (*gremio*), before an image of Our Lady which I carried with me. Concluding this act, I left the image in their houses, charging them to continue with their worship and devotion. . . ." After this initial assault, the bishop named a specific clergyman to each of the cabildos to go to them on Sundays and Holy Days and teach them Christian doctrine. He also appointed each cabildo in charge of a particular virgin that it was to venerate under the direction of a clergyman.[15]

This marvelous passage gives us all the material we need to imagine the development of santería: ethnic associations, African dances, obtuse clergymen, and worship before Catholic images. When we know that the *cabildos* were also carnival associations (*comparsas*) that played rhythms and danced "each according to its own *nación*," the picture of a Yoruba religion under the influence of Catholicism is in focus.

Bishop Morel's rather superficial catechesis of the *cabildos* makes us ask the question of the depth of Catholic influence on the religious life of the slaves. We may well wonder about the work of the Jesuit Pedro Claver (1580–1654), who is said to have baptized over 300,000 slaves. Jesuit historian Edward Reynolds describes one of Claver's catechetical methods on the docks of Cartagena: "He taught them, too, with pictures, and especially with one: a representation of Christ on the Cross, with his blood being gathered by a priest below, who, in turn, poured it over Negro neophytes. On one side of the picture were the happy Negroes who had accepted baptism; on the other were the miserable ones who had refused it."[16]

We can only imagine how Yoruba slaves would interpret this catechesis or what truths of Christian dogma they would derive from it. For his exemplary, selfless mission to the slaves, Claver was canonized in 1888. How much more usual must have been this scene described by Ralph Korngold:

> A hundred or so Negroes freshly arrived from Africa would be herded into a church, whips cracked and they were ordered to kneel. A priest followed by the acolytes and carrying a basin of holy water walked slowly down the aisle, and with vigorous swings of the aspergillum, scattered water over the heads of the crowd, chanting in Latin. The whips cracked again, the slaves rose from their knees and emerged into the light, converts to Christianity.[17]

The irony of this passage rests on calling the slaves "converts" because of the cruel impersonality of their baptism and their obvious lack of understanding of the theological meaning of the sacrament. But the irony also points to wider and important differences between the religious worldviews of Catholicism and Protestantism.

The idea of conversion in Catholicism has always laid more stress on ceremony than on experience. Catechesis, in all New World missionals, is a stage of evangelization after baptism.[18] As the practice of infant baptism implies, entry into the Roman church is not dependent on knowledge of the Bible, theological understanding, or emotional experience. Whatever the psychological disposition of the slaves receiving baptism, the Catholic church argued that they had made a genuine spiritual transition because of the church's faith in the sacramental efficacy of baptism.

This ritual interpretation of Catholic baptism can be contrasted with Protestant models of catechesis. Catholicism opened a "wide gate" to entrants, admitting all who were sacramentally initiated. Protestantism, on the other hand, opened a "narrow gate" to its prospective entrants. Conversion in the Protestant countries of the New World generally entailed a personal conversion experience. A convert would be expected to show a sincere commitment to the example of Jesus and a working knowledge of Scripture. Those who could not make this commitment could not be truly "saved," "born again," or "Christian." Entry into Protestant Christianity required a transformation—in Herskovits's terms, an acculturation—that Catholic Christianity did not.

The "wide gate" of Catholic Christianity may be seen in a different way. The popular piety of Cuban Catholicism was centered almost exclusively on the veneration of saints. Unless he or she were quite educated, the average Cuban knew a good deal more about the saints than about the gospels. Children learned their catechism through pious stories about the saints. Time was reckoned by the cycles of saints' feasts. Every city, town, village, *barrio,* and person was named for a patron saint. Havana's full name is San Christobal de la Havana; Matanza is San Carlos Alcazar de Matanza. Even the sugar mills were named after saints—Purisima Concepcion, San Martin, Santa Teresa.

Special holy images of saints were housed in shrines, the object of pilgrimage. Copies could be found in every home. The wealthy displayed robed statues, the poor colored lithographs. Churches nearly burst with reredoses, banks of saints' images on special altars throughout the buildings. Before each image burned candles signaling special intentions. Petitioners knelt before them reciting prayers handed down orally and known to be efficacious.

This hagiocentric, or saint centered, piety was the Catholicism that Yoruba slaves were enjoined to practice when they met their fates in Cuba. The ritualism of this piety provided enormous symbolic opportunities for the Yoruba.

This explosion of ritual symbolism may well be contrasted with the Protestant piety of the New World, which tended to be anti-iconic and centered on the Bible, or bibliocentric. The word rather than the image was primary, and slaves brought into Protestant cultures found their bearings in the biblical stories of exile and exodus. The Bible formed the mold for Africanity and a spirit-filled religion of prophesy and ecstacy emerged in black Protestantism, a spirtualism grounded in the teachings of the Holy Book.

The austerity of Protestant ritual symbolism brought Africans to a religiosity based on the power of the word and the invisible workings of the spirit. The variety of ritual symbolism in Catholic folk piety brought Africans to a religiosity of segmentation and correspondence, publicly Catholic and privately African.

The ethnohistorical and sociological factors isolated by Herskovits and Bastide show us how Yoruba religion was transformed into santería in Cuba. Bastide stresses the fact that slavery destroyed African families and social structures and so the interrelationships between Yoruba society and Yoruba religion.[19] Without Yoruba towns there could be no Yoruba chiefs and kings; without Yoruba families there could be no ancestors and so no societies devoted to their veneration. There are some traces of these ancestral elements in Cuba. Ortiz tells us that the old *cabildos* elected kings, buried their dead, and wore masks at carnival processions.[20] In New York today, the *egun* are remembered in every litany of the *moyuba* invocation, and divination frequently advises communication and sacrifice to a *muerto*, a deceased relative. But these ac-tivities take place in a very different social structure than nineteenth-century Yorubaland.[21]

In my sketch of Yoruba religion in chapter 1, I divided Yoruba religious experience into three categories of *ashe*—ancestors, *orishas*, and Ifa. By the loss of the social world of the African motherland, the entire ancestral complex of Yo-ruba religion was required either to disappear or to become practicable in another context. Since the Lucumi were forced into a social structure organized and legitimated by the Cath-olic church, the practices once appropriate to the Yoruba ancestors were transformed into the Catholic cult of the dead. Catholicism defined the Lucumi dead because it defined the society of the Lucumi living.

The *orisha* cults and Ifa, on the other hand, were rela-tively independent of the. Yoruba clan system and, conse-quently, survived the destruction of Yoruba society wrought by slavery. The cults to the *orisha* and Ifa could be carried to the New World in the minds of *olorishas* and *babalawos* and regenerated in forms unassimilable by Cuban society and the Catholic church. Bastide once again shows us that these, too, did not survive the middle passage without change. Without families, without lineages, without freedom, the African *orisha* cults collapsed into a single community. Whereas in Yoru-baland each deity would have a separate worship community, in Cuba all the deities came to be worshiped by one com-munity. Bastide notes that this process gave birth to what is known in Brazil as the *shire*, the holy order of *orisha* invocation that every community forges for itself.[22]

In concluding this ethnohistorical treatment of santería inspired by Herskovits and Bastide, I want to stress the im-portance of the European religions on the survival of African religions. Santería survived because of the nature of Yoruba religion, because of the social environment of colonial Cuba, and because of the qualities of Catholic folk piety. My argument is that Protestantism, by requiring a sincere, personal conversion and biblical language, demanded more of Africans in religious change. They had to pass a "narrow gate" in order to set much of African worship into biblical patterns.

Catholicism, on the other hand, required little of the slaves beyond attendance at the sacraments. Their inner dispositions, their hearts and minds, were in the *cabildos*, where Africanity was tolerated and sometimes encouraged by colonial officials.

Finally, the Catholicism of colonial Cuba was perhaps not so terribly unlike the religion of the Yoruba homeland. The emphasis on ritual, on a remote God and active, petitionable intermediaries, on blessed objects and the tangible presence of the miraculous, was not entirely foreign to Yoruba ritual expression. Catholicism offered a world of overt symbolism that could be translated into African meanings.[23] The saints provided symbols behind which the *orishas* could live on. The more symbolically austere traditions of Protestantism did not have this panoply of sacred objects for Africans to identify and reinterpret. Catholic symbolism provided a haven for the *orishas*, symbolic building blocks to recreate the way of the *orishas* in the New World.

Herskovits called the process of change that Africans endured in the New World acculturation and defined it as follows: "Acculturation comprehends those phenomena which result when groups of individuals having different cultures come into continuous, first-hand contact, with subsequent changes in the original cultural patterns of either or both groups."[24] He has been criticized for seeing the process only in terms of the minority culture coming to accept the ways of the majority, but his definition shows that the process of shaping a religion such as santería is much more complex and creative than that. Perhaps Fernando Ortiz described it better as transculturation since the process of cultural borrowing goes both ways.[25] This may have been easier for whites to see in Cuba, where blacks have been visibly active in national politics and arts since the war of independence at the close of the nineteenth century. It is also clear to Cubans that the various forms of national music—rumba, mambo, chachacha, and guaguacoa—were all part of the recreational and religious life of the *cabildos* before they emerged into Havana nightclubs.[26]

What Herskovits shows—and this is his greatest gift in writing *The Myth of the Negro Past*—is that the United States has this African heritage too. It is less obvious than Cuba's for all the ethnohistorical factors that we have gone over in this chapter. Herskovits shows us that, despite the Eurocentricism of educated Americans, the United States is a Creole country, and it is our African heritage that most distinguishes us from Europe. Our language, our music, the way we move, are all "Africanisms." The denial of our Africanity is the great myth that Herskovits succeeds in exposing.

Since the Cuban revolution of 1959, the United States has seen a reinfusion of Africanity into its melting pot. Thousands of *santeros* have come as exiles, bringing the *orishas* to America again. This has meant a second, if less brutal, transplantation and a second acculturation for Yoruba religion. This time an entirely new set of ethnohistorical factors has come into play as *santeros* acquire North American culture and Americans feel the impact of *santería*.

The presence of the *orishas* is already clear in the bilingual worlds of New York and Miami. *Botánicas* flourish; intellectuals and professionals are becoming proud initiates. Galleries sponsor shows of *orisha*-inspired art, and musicians incorporate the *orishas' toques* into popular songs.

We must wait, however, to see where and when the *orishas* may emerge to mount America at large. For now, we must move beyond the ethnohistorical perspective, to see *santería* as something more than a collection of Africanisms preserved because of peculiar environmental variables. *Santería* survived because people willed it to live and found in it the strength to meet terrible trials. The miracle of *santería* lies in the courage of the people who refused to allow slavery of the body become slavery of the spirit.[27]

11

SYMBIOSIS

It is always difficult and sometimes impossible for a white person to understand the experience of black people. Racial attitudes and prejudices lie deep in the American psyche, and the best intentions can still produce stereotypes and distortions. As a white researcher, I have struggled with the limitations of my background in understanding the world of santería. Santería is the distillate of the experience of thousands of people who have suffered a great deal at the hands of white people. It is impossible for someone who has not experienced something of that suffering to comprehend it. Herskovits has shown us that all Americans can claim an African cultural heritage, but I am still searching for a perspective that will interpret santería as truthfully as a black writer might.

Yet, because santería is a hybrid, a "syncretism" of black and white worlds, it invites the white observer to make parallels and correspondences with his or her own experience. And, because santería comes from a Latin culture not so rigidly set into racial polarities, it presents unique opportunities for white participation.

I think that I have found a way toward trying to understand the struggle of santería by seeing the slaves and freedmen who kept the religion alive as heroes in a great struggle for freedom. To keep such a tradition alive shows a heroic resistance to the spirit-crushing forces of racism and poverty. If we see the slaves only as victims and interpret their religion only as compensation for economic suffering, we will miss something fundamental about the lives of Africans in the Americas. We must be careful not to let the inhumanity of slavery blind us to the humanity of the slaves. By reacting to the horrors of slavery with guilt or anger, we may miss the miraculous survival of the spirit in the midst of that suffering. As they were worked to death in an alien world, African men and women built a spiritual oasis where there was power, respect, and love. Slave life had a continuity and integrity. Slaves learned trades, raised families, and formed friendships and fraternities. They found moments of joy and peace. This is a magnificent achievement in the brutal world of nine-teenth-century Cuba and continues to be one in the twentieth-century Bronx. By seeing slaves and their descendants as the heroes behind this achievement, I believe that we come closer to understanding santería.

The role of santería in this struggle for justice is complex. Did the world of the *orishas* offer an illusory peace, an opiate to dull the pain of powerlessness? Karl Marx summarized this problem in the famous aphorism, "Religious suffering is the expression of real suffering and at the same time the protest against real suffering."[1] Did *santeros,* in order to escape the terrible reality of enslavement, escape into a fantasy world of powerful *orishas*? Or did their faith in the *orishas* give them the strength to protest the real suffering of racist exploitation?

Nearly every scholar who has looked at this problem has agreed with Marx that the role of religion in social change is ambivalent.[2] Religions both promote and retard the struggle of the poor for equality. By affirming the existence of another world, religions take the focus off this one. Yet the belief in eternal powers provides a critical perspective on temporal ones.

North American slaveholders were well aware of this ambiguity. They were frequently reluctant to allow slaves to hear the Gospel for fear of instilling them with dangerous ideas of equality and brotherly love. When slaves were evangelized, there is plenty of evidence that white preachers would select Bible readings particularly oriented toward the Christian virtues of submissiveness and obedience.[3] Blacks, of course, saw through this sham, and black preachers focused on the liberating theme of the exodus. They recognized themselves as captives to an unjust civil power and oriented their hopes to liberation. The fact that they believed that God was their deliverer did not mean that they shrank from the struggle themselves. None less than Frederick Douglass was inspired toward his quest for freedom by the radical message of such spiritual verses as "Run to Jesus" and "I am bound for the land of Canaan."[4]

In the Latin New World, the Christianity preached to the slaves by white priests also emphasized heavenly bliss and earthly obedience. Antonio Nicolas, duke of Estrada and himself a priest, wrote a missional for Cuban slaves that likened the economy of salvation to the workings of a sugar mill—*La explicacion de la doctrina cristiana acomodada a la capacidad de los negros bozales.* Here the daily round of mill life was presented as an allegory of the dramas of sin, judgment, and salvation. The sugar mill was likened to purgatory, where the soul of the good slave was refined, like the sugar, from its impurities. The soul of the bad slave was like the burned sugar, lost forever, while the good soul went to heaven as the refined sugar went to the dryers.[5]

In chapter 2, we have seen that Cuban slaves resisted this grotesque identification of the Christian message with sugar interests. They destroyed machinery and burned cane fields. They escaped in great numbers to form the independent societies of *cimarrónes* so feared by the planters. And they rose up in revolts throughout Cuban history.

Research has not shown whether these movements were crystallized or inspired by African deities, though examples of this are frequent in other New World societies. The Haitian revolution is said to have begun with a sacred oath sworn at a *vodun* rite.[6] The present-day Rastafarian brethren await an African Christ to lead his people in the overthrow of corrupt, white Babylon.[7] In the United States, Denmark Vesey and Nat Turner were inspired by religious visions to strike against slaveholders.[8]

Africans used religion to strike at oppressors in still more direct ways. Esteban Montejo remembers Kongo sorcery in the Cuban sugar mills of the late nineteenth century:

> A *nganga*, or large pot was placed in the center of the patio. The powers were inside the pot: the saints. People started drumming and singing. They took offerings to the pot and asked for health for themselves and their brothers and peace among themselves. They also made *enkangues*, which were charms of earth from the cemetery; the earth was made into little heaps in four corners, representing the points of the universe. Inside the pot they put a plant called starshake, together with corn straw to protect the men. When a master punished a slave, the others would collect a little earth and put it in the pot. With the help of this earth they could make the master fall sick or bring some harm upon his family, for so long as the earth was inside the pot the master was imprisoned there and the Devil himself couldn't get him out.[9]

Some might interpret this symbolic aggression as compensating for the slaves' inability to control their lives, a cathartic release of frustration into harmless ritual, until it is learned that Lucumi and Kongo sorcerers knew full well the somatic properties of herbs. The pharmacoepia of African-derived religions is full of poisons and their antidotes, and slaveholders were terrified of their power.[10]

But resistance need not always be armed or lethal to be resistance. The very act of keeping alive an alternative religion such as santería is an act of resistance, a refusal to capitulate to the ideology of slavery and the selective Christianity that supported it. *Santeros* would acknowledge the extent of the power of the white world; they would become public Catholics. But they would not succumb to it. They would use the symbols of their public religion to maintain a private world of blackness, a world of African power against which the white world was only a pale translation.

Esteban Montejo writes of his experience on the plantations:

> In this country Catholicism always seems to get mixed up with magic somewhere along the way. This is a fact. There is no such thing as Catholicism pure and simple. The rich people were Catholics, but they also paid heed to witchcraft from time to time. And the overseers were really impressed by it, they didn't dare take their eyes off the Negro magic men for a second, because they knew that if the Negroes wanted they could split their skulls open. Lots of people here tell you that they are Catholic and Apostolic. I don't believe a word of it! Here almost everyone has their little missal and their stick. No person is one thing pure and simple in this country, because all the religions got mixed together. The African brought his, which is the stronger one, and the Spaniard brought his, which isn't so strong, but you should respect them all.[11]

This ability of *santeros* to maintain two religious world-views is sometimes called syncretism. It is usually used with negative connotations to mean a mixture of religious ideas without an inner integrity.[12] Caribbean religions such as santería or Haitian *vodun* are often cited as examples of syncretism because the religions involved have such different histories and because the historical materials about them are relatively recent and full. Herskovits, in his classic paper "African Gods and Catholic Saints in New World Negro Belief," wrote of syncretism as the religious expression of acculturation, producing a "synthesis between African aboriginal patterns and the European traditions to which they have been exposed."[13] By seeing the process as a fusion of religious ideas, Herskovits misses the creative and self-conscious decisions that underly santería syncretism. The French anthropologist Alfred Metraux recognizes this limitation in the interpretation of Haitian *vodun*. He writes, "No one has raised the question whether the voodooist ranks the beliefs which he holds from his African ancestors on the same level as those which he has derived from the whites."[14] The identifications between gods and saints, says Metraux, are essentially an afterthought, for "in most cases there has been no real assimilation or common identity. The equivalence of gods and saints only exists insofar as the voodooist has used pictures of saints to represent his own gods."[15]

It is my opinion that *santeros* see the chromolithographs as pictures of the *orishas* in the act of possessing human mediums. Some of the gestures, postures, and emblems of the Catholic saints in the lithographs have been taken over by *santeros* as attitudes of the *orishas* when they "mount" their devotees in possession trance. Thus, the lithographs are seen to portray *caminos*, "ways," "roads," of the *orishas* as they manifest themselves in the world of human beings. This explains why *santeros* see no problem with the fact that the male *orishas* are represented by female—and, for that matter, white—saints. When *santeros* say that the pale virgin that Catholics know as Saint Barbara is Shango, they are saying that what we see is a picture of a *camino* of Shango, Shango incarnating himself through a pale white woman who is his vehicle.[16]

The correspondence between saint and *orisha* in santería is a way for *santeros* to live in two worlds, European and African. It is a mental bridge between their public and private religions. It serves to deflect the censure of the ignorant and help sincere seekers to relate religious experiences.

But it is no more than a bridge. To express this relationship between worldviews Bastide uses the phrase "mosaic syncretism," indicating a juxtaposition of different cultural elements to form an integrated whole.[17] The Haitian-American scholar Leslie Desmangles uses the word "symbiosis" to show how *vodun* and Catholicism coexist without merging in Haiti.[18]

Bastide's and Desmangles's ideas of mosaic syncretism and symbiosis are more specific than mere mixture and more complex than a simple fusion of religious traditions. Rather, they seek principles of structural differentiation and harmony between African and Christian religions in the New World. In *The African Religions of Brazil,* Bastide shows that religious symbiosis begins on the ecological level, that is, the coexistence of African and European religious elements in space and time. He writes, "The defining characteristic of the ecological space is juxtaposition. Material objects, being rigid, cannot merge: they are located side by side within the same framework."[19]

In santería, we have seen that the *fundamentos,* the sacred *orisha* stones, are kept inside cabinets while the statues of the Catholic saints are outside, atop the cabinet or on shelves and pedestals throughout the house. During santería ceremonies, the stones are brought from the *santero's* home to the *ile* to be nourished with sacrifices, while the Catholic images are never fed. In general, *santeros* worship before the Catholic images in the Catholic manner, reciting prayers in Spanish, and before the African images in the African manner, using Lucumí.[20]

Bastide argues further that the ecological conditions of slavery forced slaves into temporal as well as spatial symbiosis. "They had, at all costs, to shift their existing ceremonies to days on which work was not required of them—which meant, in effect, accepting the Gregorian calendar."[21] In Cuba, the feasts of the Catholic saints were the occasions for the celebrations of many African-derived rites to the corresponding *orishas.* We have seen that 4 October, the feast of Saint Francis, is celebrated as that of Orula, the *orisha* of divination. On 4 December, the feast of Saint Barbara, annual rites for Shango are celebrated. Yet we can still see that these feasts have not entirely merged in the thought of *santeros*. The Christian and African celebrations never take place simultaneously, and one never suffices for the other. On the feast of one's patron *orisha*, one must attend both mass and the ceremonies of the *ile*. Many santería ceremonies take place on Saturday nights, and many members of the *ile* attend mass the next morning.

This symbiosis of ritual life was a conscious creation of Yoruba men and women responding to terrible stress. Forced into Catholic social and religious patterns, they had to adapt their representations of sacred space and time to fit European patterns. At first, this was probably no more than an adaptive strategy to preserve Yoruba cultural and religious integrity amid the erosive effects of slave society. However, what began as a pretense of Catholic worship in order to maintain the way of the *orishas* gradually became the religious mosaic that Bastide speaks of, a careful organization of Yoruba and Catholic elements into a meaningful whole. Bastide summarizes the devotees' thought on this mosaic:

> In essence, the argument runs, there is only one universal religion, which acknowledges the existence of one unique God and creator. However, this God is too remote from mankind for the latter to enter into direct contact with him: therefore "intermediaries" are necessary—Catholic saints or angels of the Old Testament for Europeans, *orisha* or *vodun* for the Negroes. Though this universal religion takes on local forms varying according to race and ethnic group, such variations are not fundamental. In any case, one can always "translate" one religion into another.[22]

This is the foundation for all efforts at comparative religion and interreligious dialogue, and I find it fascinating that the Lucumi were carrying it out in nineteenth-century Cuba. Passed off as naive "syncretism" by Western scholars, it is, in fact, a sophisticated attempt to account for the possibility of truth in multiple forms. It establishes principles for correspondence between religions, exploring the ways in which they are similar and in which they are different.

For the *santero*, the *orishas* and saints are identical in that they derive their power from one source, a power so beyond categorization that it can be conceived only as a unity. They are different in the ways that people of different cultures approach them. Lydia Cabrera told me that the old *santeros* that she knew in Cuba used to speak of Catholicism as *el camino de los blancos* and santería as *el camino de los negros* (the way of the whites and the way of the blacks). When we remember that *camino*, "way," "road," is a special term for different manifestations of the same *orisha*, we can see that *santeros* feel that the *orishas* are identical in the abstract and different in the concrete rituals that invoke them.

This distinction was made even clearer for me when I asked a senior *santera* in Philadelphia about the difference between the *orishas* and the saints. She thought about it carefully and answered, "Los santos no comen," "The saints don't eat."

Following Bastide's idea of religions as translations of each other, we might say that the way of the *orishas* and the way of Catholicism are two different languages and that the *santero* is competent in both. He or she "thinks" in Lucumi but "speaks" either "*orisha*" or "saint," depending on the ritual context. *Santeros* are thus bilingual or bicultural or bireligious.[23] They are convinced of the essential theological unity of the Christian and African spirits but choose to approach them in distinctly Christian or African ways, depending on their context. Each system of behavior is like a piece of the mosaic, separable but bound together by correspondences into the total picture of santería. Santería allows *santeros* to live in two worlds—the *camino* of the whites and the *camino* of the blacks.

The symbiosis of *orisha* and saint, of Africa and Europe, is the *santeros'* solution to Marx's problem of accommodation and resistance. It is at once elegant, creative, and clever.

Santeros accommodated themselves to the white world by conforming their calendar to the Roman festivals, by participating in Catholic rites, and by using Catholic icons to represent their ideas of spiritual power. They, in fact, became Catholics. But by steadfastly remembering that Catholicism was only a correspondence to the way of the *orishas,* a translation of a deeper, more puissant way of worship, they resisted the limiting and racist definition of themselves held by white Catholic society.

Marx's critique of religion depends on an ontology, a belief or position about what is truly real. The "real world" for Marx is the struggle of classes, and the only reality that the world of religious belief has is as an ideology in that struggle. I have been arguing that, even if the world of the *orishas* is a fiction, a magnificent creation of the African imagination, *santeros* found in it a key to resisting oppression. If they believed themselves to be spiritually free, they were genuinely free in important ways. Marx would answer that this spiritual freedom was merely "flowers" concealing the "chain" of class oppression. But if the world of the *orishas* is in fact a genuine world, then Marx's aphorism is turned on its head. Marx's opiate is then a "psychedelic," a way of life that expands consciousness rather than restricting it to shield the believer from pain. If the *orishas* are real, then the world of suffering and racism is to be explained and solved in terms of the *orishas.*

Santeros believe that the *orishas* are real, and so it is essential that we consider this reality if we are to understand santería. My final chapter, then, attempts to look at santería as a *santero* would. Once again, santería is a miracle, but not a miracle because it survived slavery, and not a miracle because *santeros* heroically resisted racism. It is a miracle because it is true.

12

THE RELIGION

As a religion, santería needs a special kind of interpretation that will do justice to the spiritual world of its devotees. Religions offer their practitioners a unique dimension of experience that motivates them to interpret their whole lives by it. If we are truly to understand santería, we must take this special world seriously. We must attempt to see it as *santeros* do—alive, powerful, real.

But our attempt to make this leap of understanding runs into a host of problems of method. In the same way that we asked whether whites can interpret the experience of blacks, we wonder whether non-*santeros* can interpret santería. Must we believe in santería in order to understand it? If we leave our objectivity behind, will our interpretation of santería be only a projection of our own religious experience? A variety of scholars have wrestled with these questions, and I want to show how their ideas contribute to the interpretation of santería.

UNDERSTANDING A RELIGION

In their hopes to create a science of human behavior, anthropologists and sociologists have worked to develop methods that will screen the subjective experience of the researcher from the data being collected and described. American anthropologists often speak of two ways of categorizing and interpreting data to arrive at objectivity in cultural description: the emic and the etic.[1] The goal of emic ethnography is to present cultural data purely in the categories of thought used by a member of that culture. While the ethnographer must systematize those categories and present them in English, the end result would produce an ethnography with which the "native" would agree and that would be able to predict "native" exegesis of new data. Etic analysis, on the other hand, seeks to interpret cultural data by means of the categories applied by the researcher from his or her own, presumably Western, culture.

Obviously, both these methods work together to help the outsider understand santería. Alone or together, they expand our knowledge of something strange to us as outsiders, something that eludes our grasp and needs to be understood. But they miss something too, something at the heart of the ceremony. The *bembe* is also something that is not strange to us; it calls on something that the outsider and the *santero* share. When the outsider participates in a *bembe,* he or she also experiences something that is crucial to examine in order to interpret the ceremony correctly.

The German sociologist Max Weber recognized that the objective interpretation of human meaning necessarily involved the subjective viewpoint of the observer.[2] Weber argued that we can understand these meanings only by empathy, by feeling that they conform to ideal types of meaning shared by all human beings. We have to make the unverifiable assumption that we are able to understand others before we can make verifiable statements about what we have understood about them.

When we turn to religious behavior, the necessity of empathy takes on particular challenges. The German-American scholar Joachim Wach speaks of a "hermeneutic circle," an interpretive double bind that demands that the observer share religious meaning with those he or she is attempting to understand. Acknowledging a debt to historian Wilhelm Dilthey, Wach writes,

Concretely stated, the religious content of myth cannot be found alone in a careful and thorough, though necessary, analysis of its ideological elements and motives; rather, the entire personality of him who studies and understands is spoken to. If he wishes to understand the attitude from which the mythological faith and custom have issued, he must respond. An inner aliveness and broadness is necessary if we actually wish to understand other religions.

. . . Hermeneutics demands that he who wishes to understand other religions must have a sense for religion and in addition the most extensive knowledge and training possible.[3]

Following Wach, I believe that santería, as a religion, requires this "sense" of religion in the observer in order for him or her to understand it properly. It is impossible for the outsider to know what santería means to the *santero*, but this religious sense in the observer can only bring him or her closer to what a *santero* believes than attempts at detached objectivity.

In his classic study of religious experience, *The Idea of the Holy*, the German theologian Rudolf Otto shows little patience with scholarly detachment in the study of religion:

The reader is invited to direct his mind to a moment of deeply-felt religious experience, as little as possible qualified by other forms of consciousness. Whoever cannot do this, whoever knows no such moments in his experience, is requested to read no farther; for it is not easy to discuss questions of religious psychology with one who can recollect the emotions of his adolescence, the discomforts of indigestion, or, say, social feelings, but cannot recall any intrinsically religious feelings.[4]

Perhaps Otto goes too far with this jibe at scientific detachment, but his point is well taken. Some level of empathy and identification with the religious experiences of others is a prerequisite for understanding their religion.[5] One does not have to believe·in santería in order to understand it, but one must be willing to believe in something. The observer must find the empathy to see that *santeros* feel as deeply about santería as the observer does about his or her most deeply held convictions. As *santeros* have repeatedly told me, the *orishas* will respond only if the seeker gives something of himself or herself to them. So this interpretation of santería is indeed a projection of my own religious experience, but it is a projection shaped by years of listening to Padrino, the drums, and the *orishas.*

If santería is to be understood as a religion, beyond the social and cultural forces that have shaped it, we must develop an idea of religion as a category in itself. What is religion besides a cultural focus or a means of social differentiation and cohesion?

Rudolf Otto argued that the origin and essence of religion is to be found in deep emotional experiences that he called "numinous."[6] A numinous experience is uniquely religious, shared in greater and lesser intensities by all religious people of every culture and historical epoch. The heart of religion for Otto is an awesome, numinous experience of a "wholly other" reality, a holy or sacred dimension of existence that stands apart from and beyond the ordinary world in which we live.

The historian of religions Mircea Eliade expands on Otto's ideas by seeing religion as a dialectic between these realms of experience—the sacred, eternal world of the gods and the profane, ordinary world of time and change.[7] The sacred world provides the models or archetypes for meaningful action in the profane world of ordinary life. Eliade writes,

> The point to be emphasized is that, from the be-
> ginning, religious man sets the model he is to
> attain on the trans-human plane, the plane re-
> vealed by his myths. One becomes truly a man

only by conforming to the teachings of the
myths, that is by imitating the gods.[8]

The more religious man is, the more paradig-
matic models does he possess to guide his attitudes and actions.[9]

Myths symbolize the content of the sacred world. Rituals, by
aligning human actions with mythic models, allow human
beings to approach the sacred world. Religion, then is a relation to a sacred world, an attempt to align human actions
with those of a world of eternal significance. As a religion,
santería can be understood in the light of this dialectic of
sacred and profane. Santería is the way of the saints, the way
that *santeros* living in the profane, ordinary world of the Bronx
approach the sacred, eternal world of the *orishas* at Ile-Ife.

SANTERÍA ONTOLOGY

The sacred world of santería is motivated by *ashe*. *Ashe* is
growth, the force toward completeness and divinity. The Bel-
gian missionary Placide Tempels called this view of the world
an ontology of dynamism, that is, a belief that the real world
is one of pure movement.[10] In fact, the real world is one not
of objects at all but of forces in continual process. *Ashe* is the
absolute ground of reality. But we must remember that it is a
ground that moves and, so, no ground at all. To conceive this
ground, in order to speak of it as something rather than nothing, *santeros* speak of Olodumare, the Owner of Heaven, the
Owner of all Destinies. Olodumare is the object of *ashe*, the
ultimate harmony and direction of all forces.

As one enters more deeply into santería, one sees this
vision of *ashe* with increasing clarity. All things that we are
accustomed to call beings are, in reality, *caminos*, ways of *ashe*
that can be liberated and channeled by those who understand
them. The person of wisdom, the true *santero*, learns to work

with these forces. By words and actions, *ashe* can be awakened in what seem to be objects and people to bring about the fulfillment of their destinies. Stones, leaves, animals, and people are vibrations brought into harmony by *santeros* to further them on their road in the way of Olodumare.

Ashe is a current or flow, a "groove" that initiates can channel so that it carries them along their road in life. The prayers, rhythms, offerings, tabus of santería tune initiates into this flow. They are lifted out of the self-absorption and frustration of ordinary life into the world of power where everything is easy because all is *ashe*, all is destiny.

The *santero* reaches this world by movement. When I have attended santería ceremonies, I have been reminded of those old British anthropologists pronouncing on "savage" religion as "danced religion."[11] For, in spite of themselves, they were right. What they did not know is the profound religious insight that African dancing reveals. Santería is a danced religion because dancing expresses the fundamental dynamism of *ashe*. Words, even a religious encyclopedia like Ifa, cannot express the mystery. The world is a dance. Its meaning lies in its constant movement. The dance is the expression of this mystery and more: it is its technology.

Ashe is liberated and channeled through dancing; the person and the community are brought to the source, the real world. In Eliade's terms, the dancers are brought back to the real time of the beginnings, the time of the myths when the *orishas* lived at Ile-Ife. The dancers become contemporaries of the gods.

The technology of santería dance may be neurobiological. Movement, rhythm, adrenaline, exhaustion, may trigger hypnotic states of mind that were imprinted in the brain during initiation.[12] The insight that *santeros* bring to this explanation is the ontological claim of the religious—that the special states of mind brought on by dance reveal the world as it truly is, a world of unfiltered *ashe*. *Orisha* consciousness is true consciousness, and our ordinary view of the world is derived from it.

This ontological claim comes through in the derivation of the word *orisha*. The Yoruba theologian E. B. Idowu thinks that *orisha* is a contraction of the words *ori,* "head," and *sha,* "source," yielding something like "head source."[13] When we remember that *ori* is that ancestral aspect of ourselves that chose our destiny before we were born, an *ori-sha* would be the source of this self. Abstracted further, we may say that an *orisha* is the source of that consciousness that makes us what we are.

Santeros in New York have told me that an *orisha* is *el dueño de tu cabeza,* the "lord of your head." This may mean little more than a deity above and beyond oneself, a lord in the medieval sense of one's social superior. Yet I am led to think that, if this deity is lord over one's "head," one's consciousness, then the language of consciousness is the most appropriate way to interpret the meaning of *orisha*. The lord of one's head is the personification of a higher, truer consciousness of the world. Through the images of deities, santería is presenting a precise and profound ontology of consciousness.

Santería teaches not only that *ashe* is dynamic but also that it can be channeled into types. There are innumerable kinds of *ashe* as there are innumerable kinds of people in the world. A monotheistic perspective sees these as "hypostases," "ministers," "intermediaries," "manifestations," of one force.[14] A polytheistic perspective recognizes intrinsic differences among our experiences of the world and sees these types representing the variety and possible ways of being in the world. While these experiences are theoretically infinite, there must be a limited number of types to be intelligible and useful as a typology of the sacred world. These are the *orishas,* the types of *ashe*.

Santeros have several overlapping ways of classifying the *orishas*. For example, *orishas* can be hot and cool. Shango, Ogun, and Babaluaye work through the fire of lightning, forge, and fever to heat up the *ashe* of the devotee in order to force change in the world. Osanyin, Inle, and Oshun cool through leaves, herbs, and fresh water, calming the hot head that impedes the devotee's vision of destiny.

There are also *orishas* of the sky and *orishas* of the earth. Obatala the sculptor and Orula the diviner work with Olodumare on high to shape and interpret our destinies. Nana and Babaluaye roam the earth choosing whom they will for illnesses, punishing or calling them to service.

There are *orishas* of the forest and *orishas* of the town. Osanyin is the lord of the forest, the genius of the wild leaves from which all the efficacy of santería ritual derives. Eleggua, Ogun, and Oshosi are hunters who walk together outside the boundaries of the community. They are fearless and fearsome because they know the secrets of an unknown world. Within the town are the royal *orishas*: Obatala, king of Ife; Shango, king of Oyo; and Ogun, king of Ire. The royal *orishas* command the *ashe* of seniority, the power of connection to the world of the beginnings, Ile-Ife.

Finally, there is Eleggua and all the other *orishas*. Eleggua is the restless outsider betwixt and between worlds. He overturns order and, by doing so, reveals it. Ifa is the senior *orisha* of destiny and order, but Eleggua is the true *orisha* of divination because his randomness and unpredictability show the true order in the world. Out of the fall of shells and nuts, the order of our destinies becomes clear. Because Eleggua disrupts our lives, we learn the patterns that control them. *Santeros* say that Eleggua serves all the *orishas*, that each *orisha* has his or her own Eleggua. Without Eleggua and the disorder that he provokes, the *orishas* would all starve, for they would have no purpose. Human beings would have no need of them, and no sacrifices would be due them. Eleggua provides the dynamism that moves the road of life.

We have seen that santería expresses a religious ontology, that is, a belief about what is ultimately real. Reality is *ashe*, vital force, and all the objects of the world are in reality forces of *ashe* in relation to each other. The *orishas* are the major types of *ashe* expressed in the mythological language of personality and narrative. Myths, Eliade tells us, reveal how the real world works. The myths of the *orishas* are timeless stories that provide models for human beings to imitate in order to live in the real world. By imitating and repeating the timeless acts of the *orishas* in rituals, human beings can approach and align themselves with the real world of *ashe.*

THE WAY OF THE SAINTS: SANTERÍA RITUAL

Santería recognizes four principal ritual ways of approach to the world of the *orishas*: divination, sacrifice, trance, and initiation.

All santería ritual begins with divination, and all divination begins with a devotee's problem. Since *santeros* are often poor, the most pressing problems are generally very practical ones involving health, money, and love. Without the money for private physicians, and finding little but insensitivity and misunderstanding in overworked public institutions, *santeros* trust the world of the *orishas* for help with health problems. This is not to say that it is only deprivation that forces *santeros* to turn to the *orishas. Santeros* say that modern medicine treats only the symptoms of more basic spiritual problems. Padrino has told me several times that he always sends querents with medical problems to qualified doctors but that the basic problem will keep recurring until they understand that their illness is a message from the *orishas.* The same argument holds for problems of money and love. Poverty and wayward spouses are ultimately problems of the spirit, problems of the "head," which is out of tune, "not listening," to the call of the *orishas.*

It takes knowledge and insight to recognize the spiritual causes of ordinary problems, and it takes information to treat them. This is the realm of divination, the art of the awareness of destiny. Divination offers the means for interpreting the meaning of random events. With increasing subtlety and precision, Obi, *dilogun,* and Ifa divination open the devotee to the world of *ashe* by providing information. They offer models of divine action, stories of what the *orishas* and heroes did in Ile-Ife when they were faced with the same problem that querents face today. With absolute specificity, santería divination aligns human with divine action, opening the channels of *ashe*. Divination is effective because, when the querent seeks meaning in chance, he or she establishes what psychologist Carl Jung calls a "synchronous" connection between timeless meaning and the moment the querent seeks meaning.[15] The *odu* that falls for the *santería* querent was meant to fall, at that time and for that person. Divination gives the *santero* the knowledge of his or her destiny and specific models for action in order to take advantage of it.

Nearly all the problems and situations that divination reveals are resolved or furthered by deepening the devotee's relationship with the *orishas*. There is no firmer way for the devotee to show this relationship than through the symbolism of shared food, that is, in sacrifice. Sacrifice (*ebo*) creates bonds between human beings and *orishas*. It is a gift that opens up the channels of *ashe* by exchange. In divination, the *orishas* speak to human beings, diagnosing their needs and opening their destinies to fulfillment. In sacrifice, human beings respond, giving back to the *orishas* the *ashe* that is the sustenance of life.[16]

Though they are more powerful than human beings, the *orishas* are not omnipotent. Like all living things, they must be constantly nourished. A Yoruba proverb says that, without human beings, there would be no *orishas*. The *orishas* need the sacrifice and praise of human beings in order to continue to be effective.

Sacrifices can also be exchanges of another kind. The *orishas* can make terrible demands on their devotees, even to the point of threatening their lives. Sacrifices are gifts to propitiate the *orishas*, to give them the life that they need and to spare the devotee's own: *vida para vida*, say the *santeros*, life for life.

In a general sense, an *ebo* is any ceremony requested by an *orisha*, including purifying baths, feasts, or initiation ceremonies. More particularly, *ebos* are the offerings of foods requested by the *orishas* through divination. Each *orisha* has special foods that it enjoys. Yemaya, the ocean mother, prefers duck, turtle, and goat. Oshun, the lovely river maid, likes fine cakes and white hens. Ogun, the virile iron master, insists on red and white roosters. Sometimes the *odus* of divination are very specific about which foods are to be offered to which *orishas*. The *dilogun odu* called *Eyioko*, for example, prescribes special offerings for one of six possible *orishas* speaking through it, plus two parrots, two coconuts, two eggs, and two doves. The Ifa *odu ogbe meji* related by Bascom requires a sacrifice of two black hens, two pigeons, two roosters, two pots, one arrow, one leg of a deer, and one feather of a parrot.[17]

The French anthropologist Dominique Zahan calls the African attention to sacrificial detail a "choelogy," a science of libations, by which the combination of sacrificial ingredients produces powerful and effective semantic statements.[18] For *santeros*, specificity is the key to efficacy. One offers the *orisha* precisely what the *orisha* wants, where and when the *orisha* wants it, and in response to a particular situation for which the *orisha*'s *ashe* is sought.

The theory behind all santería sacrifice is that the *orishas* consume the invisible *ashe* of the sacrifices that is instilled in or, better, liberated from them through consecration, the sacred words of the *moyuba* dedication. A *santero* once told Lydia Cabrera, "La sangre para el Santo, la carne para el santero," "Blood for the saint, meat for the *santero*."[19] The *ashe* of the sacrifices is consumed invisibly in vegetable sacrifices and through the blood of the animal in animal sacrifices, which is sprinkled or poured on the fundamental symbols of the *orishas*. The blood of animals consecrated to the *orishas* strengthens their powers: once again, *vida para vida*, "life for life." When the blood is poured on the "heads" of the *orishas*, the sacred stones, or the prepared heads of the initiates, the *orisha* is fed, and the devotee shares in the *orisha*'s *ashe*.

The most dramatic and intimate approach to the world of the *orishas* is the cultivation of a sacred state of consciousness induced by the drums and dances of the *bembe*. This consciousness, sometimes called trance or spirit possession by outsiders, collapses the sacred dialogue of divination and sacrifice into a single ritual encounter. In santería trance, the channels of *ashe* are fully open as human dancers merge with divine rhythms.

It is difficult to find an English word that will describe this sacred consciousness. "Trance" connotes an inferior, suggestable state of awareness, while "spirit possession" implies to most Westerners a demonic influence. Yet santería mediums claim to remember nothing of their activities when in this altered state of awareness, so the term "trance" is not entirely unfounded. And since their behavior is controlled by the *orisha*, "possession" conveys something of the experience.

The basic problem rests on the understanding of this consciousness as religious. Santería presents an ontology of consciousness, the belief that certain states of awareness reveal the world as it truly is and that our ordinary awareness, while possessing its own validity, is dependent on this *orisha* consciousness.

If we recognize the limitations and possible misinterpretations of the word, "trance" is probably the easiest way to refer to this special awareness, especially if we remember that, for *santeros*, this "trance" is a special and genuine form of awareness.[20] *Santeros* themselves speak of *bajar el santo*, "the saint descending," or *el santo montado*, "the saint mounted," which places emphasis on the activity of the *orisha* in descending on or mounting the head of the medium. The "mounting" activity of an *orisha* refers to the medium's role as a "horse" whose activities are directed by an *orisha* rider.[21]

The most persistent misconception about trance is that it is frenzied or hysterical behavior. While the transition from ordinary to trance consciousness may involve some sudden, staggered movements among inexperienced mediums, once the *orisha* has fully mounted the medium his or her behavior becomes very precise indeed. The dances are tightly choreographed according to traditional models and are immediately recognizable to the congregation as reenactments of mythical themes. Sometimes these themes are simply gestures recalling the *orisha*'s powers, such as Ogun swinging his machete or Oshosi drawing his bow. But the dances can be elaborate pantomimed dramas that last for hours.[22] When more than one *orisha* joins a *bembe*, they reenact their mythical relationships with each other. Ogun and Shango feud, Obatala asserts his authority over Shango, and Oshun plays cruel tricks on her rival Oba.

Even more important than the dance is the incarnated *orisha*'s capacity to give advice. Throughout the course of a *bembe*, an *orisha* may favor certain devotees with warnings, admonitions, and harangues. *Santeros* have told me that incarnated *orishas* can make startlingly accurate predictions about the personal lives of devotees and that one should always take their advice. One *santera* told me that she consistently hits the lottery on the numbers that *orishas* give to her.

These patterns of *orisha* behavior occur in a particular cultural context. Mediums generally have grown up in a culture surrounded by santería and have seen many *bembes* before they have ever been "mounted" themselves. It is impossible to say whether the medium learns trance behavior or learns to be a medium for trance behavior. The Franco-Brazilian ethnologist Pierre Verger writes of Yoruba trance and initiation, "He [the initiate] carries within himself the latent image of the god, impressed at the time of initiation on a mind free of all impressions and this image is revealed and manifested when all the favorable conditions are brought together."[23]

When one is initiated into santería during the *asiento* ceremony, the *orisha* determined to be one's patron is "seated" inside one's "head." This ceremony is an incarnation in potential, which becomes realized when the *orisha* becomes manifest in the trance dance of the *bembe*. Following Verger, the American anthropologist Sheila Walker shows the complex relationship between the "head" of the devotee and the deity that mounts it by contrasting West African trance, which she characterizes as "mostly cultural," with Afro-Brazilian trance, which she argues is "cultural and psychological in equal proportions." She writes,

> In the traditional Dahomean and Yoruba cults in
> Africa only one deity was served by a devotee,

but possession by him was not expected to allow
the expression of any personal tendencies. The
benefit to the devotee was mainly the opportunity to be appreciated by others in such an exalted position. In Bahia possession by a god is
supposed to express a facet of the devotee's personality, but although there are many deities, an
individual may, in the traditional Yoruba cults,
only be possessed by one. [24]

Once again, the "place" of the *orisha* is ambiguous. Is
the *orisha* a cultural category internalized by the medium? Or
is it a psychological category emerging in culturally recognized
forms? By saying that they do not remember their behavior
during trance, *santeros* seem to deemphasize both the exalted
status of the medium and the psychological aspects of trance.
Santeros have repeatedly told me that it is not the medium
who profits from trance but the community that enjoys the
healing presence of the *orisha*. Yet observers have noted that
the amnesia of mediums absolves them of responsibility for
their trance behavior and so allows mediums special opportunities for uncensored self-expression. [25] Much of the things
incarnated *orishas* say and do is aggressive and impolite, and
they often reveal a great deal of gossip. Is trance not an opportunity for the powerless to set everyone straight?

I do not think that *santeros* would disagree with this kind
of interpretation of trance if we remember that it is not the
medium but the *orisha* who is telling the truth. What is interesting is that the outsider and the *santero* would agree that
the *orisha* is a subconscious part of the medium's personality.
The difference in the viewpoints is the ontological claim of
the *santero* that the *orisha* is the real source of the medium's
personality. For the outsider, it may be seen as a suppressed
side of the personality giving vent to antisocial feelings; for
the *santero*, it is the genuine and divine source of the personality and thus worthy of the deepest respect.

Santeros find the *orisha* both within and without. They
see it as an influence from outside the person since it takes a

ceremony to "seat" one in the devotee's head. On the other hand, since the *orisha* is consciousness itself, it can be said to emerge through the human body as its material medium. In trance this force streams through human consciousness unhindered. The huge eyes of the medium open to a light shining from within.

This special awareness is a mark or sign of a deepening relationship with the *orishas*. With divination and sacrifice, it aligns the world of human beings with the world of the *orishas* and brings the devotee toward the reality of *ashe*. This process of growth *en santo*, "in saintliness," in *ashe*, is marked by ceremonies of initiation. Initiation both recognizes wisdom and imparts knowledge. The ceremonies show to the devotee and to the community the depth of the devotee's commitment to the *orishas* and his or her mastery of the techniques of invoking *ashe*.

Santeros speak of initiation as "making" the saint, *hacer el santo*. Mercedes made Obatala and Padrino made Ifa. This making suggests an active engagement on the part of the initiate. His or her involvement with the *orisha* creates the power of that *orisha*. One "makes" an *orisha* as one makes a commitment to an *orisha*, perhaps as one "makes" love with a lover. The *orisha* is not a static symbol to be had but a moving, flowing current to be enhanced, "made" by the devotee's commitment.

Although I have been using the word *santero* to refer to all santería devotees, only those who have made the saint can be properly called *santeras* or *santeros*. Their role is revealed in the Lucumi words *iyalocha* and *babalocha*. *Iya* means both mother and wife and *baba* both father and husband. *Ocha* is *orisha*. So initiates are both mothers and wives, fathers and husbands, of the *orishas*. They serve their *orishas* as spouses and give birth to *orishas* by making them in the heads of new initiates. Thus, an *orisha* is in a continual process of rebirth, being made anew everytime an *iyalocha* gives birth to a new godchild.

There are basically two roads of initiation in *santería*, which were once explained to me as *el camino del santo* and

el camino de Orula (the way of the saint and the way of Orula).
Each road leads to a different kind of priesthood: the priesthood of the *orishas,* the *iyalocha* and *babalocha,* and the priesthood of Orula or Ifa, the *babalawo.* Each road leads to different
kinds of divination as well: *santo* prepares the head for divination by trance, and Orula prepares the mind for the insight
to interpret Ifa. While the road of *santo* is open to both men
and women, the road of Orula is available only to men. The
preponderance of *santo* initiates are women. I estimate that
there are roughly four women to every man in Padrino's *ile.*
I have been told that women are more "open" to the influence
of the *orishas* than men are, and I wonder if the symbolism of
sexual union is again the explanation. Since women are likely
to be "mounted" by men in sexual intercourse, are women's
spirits, their "heads," likely to be mounted by *orishas* in the
spiritual intercourse of trance?

The road of Orula, the path of the *babalawo* priesthood,
is open only to those few whom Ifa calls and who are willing
to undergo the arduous training to master the oracle. Most
devotees are called to the path of *santo,* the path of *orishas*
who are seated in the head. In the *asiento* ceremony, the
devotee makes the basic constellation of the most important
orishas, whichever royal courtiers are demanded by the patron
orisha, usually Obatala, Yemaya, Oshun, Shango, and often
Oya. Later, many *santeros* go on to make other *orishas,* each
with its own prayers and rituals to be mastered and special
relationships to be fostered—*orishas* such as Babaluaye, Inle,
and the Ibeji. If they are called to it, some *santeros* make a
different Ogun than the one who walks with Eleggua and
Oshosi at the devotee's door. This Ogun confers the ability
to use the sacrificial knife, *pinaldo,* in order to offer larger,
four-footed animals to the *orishas.* With each new initiation,
the devotee is brought more fully into the community of the
orishas and the real world of Ile-Ife.

When I received Eleggua and the other warrior *orishas,*
I was making my first step toward a relationship with *ashe.* I
learned some elementary Lucumi prayers in order to address
Eleggua. I learned how to offer him nonanimal sacrifices of

water, rum, tobacco, and roasted corn. I learned to listen to his responses through *obi* divination. In the beginning, this give and take was awkward and stiff. Only gradually does the formality of a ritualized relationship become a vehicle to focus sincerity. As the relationship with the warriors develops, I will be ready for more complex and specific relationships with them and with the other *orishas,* and these will involve still more complex and specific prayers and offerings. It is only through this slow process of learning and giving that the secrets of santería will be revealed.

My interpretation of santería rests on my level of initiation. Understanding the *orishas* requires both the knowledge of the techniques of invocation and the experience of relating to another personality. It requires the willingness to make the sacrifices necessary to bring to life a friendship, or a love affair, or a marriage. This is why Madrina and Padrino keep calling on me to listen to the *orishas.* Growth *en santo* requires the active engagement of the devotee. This is also why the interpretation of my experience at the *bembe* remains closed to me. Its significance cannot become apparent until I am willing to make a further commitment to the *orishas* involved. The intimacy of trance usually requires the commitment of *asiento* initiation in the same way that society sanctions the intimacy of man and woman in marriage. In order to make this commitment, one must work to learn of the ways of another and work to be able to give of oneself to another. One must work in order to love.

As a devotee grows in this love, one particular *orisha* will begin to assert itself as the devotee's patron, and it is the love of this *orisha* that will provide the devotee with his or her basic orientation in life. *Asiento,* the ceremony of seating the *orisha* in the head of the devotee, seals a fundamental bond of consciousness between human being and *orisha.* The *iyawo* Mercedes received Obatala, and so a fundamental part of her consciousness is Obatala. After the rebirth drama of *asiento,* she entered a new life as Obatala, who now "owns" her head. Surrender to this *orisha* tunes her into the real world of *ashe.*

Through the very special and secret prayers that a devotee has learned during initiation, the relationship between human being and *orisha* becomes ever deeper. The world is revealed as a theater for the interaction of invisible powers, and the *orisha* within is an infallible guide to worldly success and heavenly wisdom. The spiritual exchange between human being and *orisha* becomes increasingly more fluid. The devotee no longer must listen to the call of the *orisha* because the voice is his or her very self. The prayers, sacrifices, divinations, and dances come to be seen as the outward manifestations of inner processes. Thus, santería culminates in a mysticism of identity between *orisha* and human being, not only in the trance consciousness of the *bembe,* but in everything that the *santero* does.

One time, a distinguished *santera* named Ayorinde came to visit Padrino's *ile.* She was tall and thin and very old, but she carried herself erectly. When I was introduced to her, I had that strange sensation of having known her a long, long time. She smiled very kindly at me as if she knew my thoughts, and this only made my feelings of unsettled wonder grow. After some polite small talk with my eyes locked on hers, I dared to ask a question. I asked, "What is an *orisha?*" Her gaze never wavered. She just said softly, "I am."

NOTES

1: AFRICA

1. Some of the spectacular archaeological finds at the Yoruba city of Ife have been determined by radiocarbon tests to date from the tenth century of the common era. Frank Willett has concluded from his excavations at Ife in the 1950s and 1960s that the city has been occupied since 800 C.E. (see *Ife in the History of West African Sculpture* [London: Thames & Hudson, 1967]). For a shorter discussion of the relevance of archaeology to Yoruba history, see Frank Willett, "Archaeology," in *Sources of Yoruba History,* edited by S. O. Biobaku (Oxford: Clarendon, 1973). This valuable book examines Yoruba history from a number of viewpoints, including discussions of oral and written history, oral literature, ceremonies, language, and art.

The stylistic connections between contemporary Yoruba art and that of the prehistoric Nok civilization, which dates from the sixth century before the common era, suggest an even greater antiquity for Yoruba culture. Willett speaks of these connections in the beautifully illustrated catalog *Treasures of Ancient Nigeria* (New York: Knopf, 1980), pp. 27–28. Fellow art historian and archaeologist William Fagg is more cautious about Yoruba-Nok connections in the equally sumptuous *Yoruba Sculpture of West Africa* (New York: Knopf, 1982), p. 28. This book, edited by Bryce Holcombe with rich and detailed catalog description by John Pemberton III, contains a thorough bibliography of Yoruba art criticism.

2. For an introduction to the extent and excellence of Yoruba art, see Robert Farris Thompson, *Black Gods and Kings* (Bloomington: Indiana University Press, 1976).

3. In 1897, the Yoruba clergyman Samuel Johnson produced the first written history of Oyo from oral sources, first published as *The History of the*

Yorubas (Lagos: C.M.S. Bookshops, 1921). For a documentary survey of available written records, see Thomas Hodgkin, *Nigerian Perspectives: An Historical Anthology* (London: Oxford University Press, 1960). For an excellent short account of Oyo, see Peter Morton-Williams, "The Yoruba Kingdom of Oyo," in *West African Kingdoms in the Nineteenth Century,* edited by Daryll Forde and Phyllis Kaberry (London: Oxford University Press, 1967). See also R. S. Smith, *Kingdoms of the Yoruba* (London: Methuen, 1969). An authoritative full history of Old Oyo is R. C. C. Law's *The Oyo Empire: 1600–1836* (Oxford: Oxford University Press, 1977).

4. For a listing of the major sources for the study of Yoruba religion, see the bibliography. This study, like so many before it, is written in what is often called the "ethnographic present." This means that Yoruba religious beliefs are presented in an artificial "present tense," which tends to support the widely held misconception that African cultures have no history and never change. A second problem with this kind of presentation is that it ignores important regional differences among the Yoruba—the very word "Yoruba" is a foreign word—and so presents a false picture of unity and uniformity, supporting another popular misconception about the simplicity of "primitive" cultures. Finally, this summary of Yoruba religion builds into a system what most Yorubas do not systematize in this way, if at all.

I think that all these ethnographic sins are justified in the interests of clarity and brevity. While Yoruba religion has changed and continues to change, what follows is a reasonable portrait of that abstraction of "Yoruba religion" that is applicable throughout Yoruba history and across the regions of Yorubaland. For those who say that the word "religion" itself is an imposition of Western categories onto a non-Western culture, I have yet to find a better word to summarize and systematize the subject that interests us. If we are to write in English, we are enmeshed in Western categories, and the attempt to understand another culture in terms of those categories is legitimate and necessary. For discussions of religious change, see J. D. Y. Peel, "Religious Change in Yorubaland," *Africa,* vol. 37, no. 3 (1967); J. K. Parratt, "Religious Change in Yoruba Society: A Test Case," *Journal of Religion in Africa,* vol. 2 (1969); and J. S. Eades, *The Yoruba Today* (Cambridge: Cambridge University Press, 1980). On avenues of research on the history of Yoruba worship, see Peter R. McKenzie, "Orisa Cults in Western Nigeria, 1846–79: The Evidence of Indigenous Pastors," *Africana Marburgensia,* vol. 14, no. 1 (1981). For a critique of the cross-cultural application of the idea of "religion" from a sympathetic scholar, see Wilfred Cantwell Smith, *The Meaning and End of Religion* (New York: Macmillan, 1962). For a defense, see Robert D. Baird, *Category Formation in the History of Religions* (The Hague: Mouton, 1971).

5. Responding to the theological controversies about the role of the high god in African traditional religion, the Yoruba scholar E. B. Idowu has written a thoroughly supported argument for the centrality of Olodumare in Yoruba religious thought (see *Olodumare: God in Yoruba Belief* [London: Longmans, 1962]). As Idowu is a Christian clergyman, he may be criticized for his zeal in seeking to harmonize traditional Yoruba religion with his conviction of the truth of Christian doctrine. He has also been taken to task for what O. Ogunba considers to be his general overestimation of Yoruba piety ("Ceremonies," in *Sources of Yoruba History*, p. 90).

6. Idowu, *Olodumare*, p. 55.

7. In trying to organize the variety of possible perspectives on Yoruba religion, I am most indebted to the Franco-Brazilian ethnographer Pierre Verger (esp. "The Yoruba High God: A Review of the Sources," *Odu*, n.s., vol. 2, no. 2 [1966]). He argues that *ashe* is the central organizing feature of the Yoruba worldview and the ground for the Yoruba idea of God. He writes of *ashe*, "It embraces all mystery, all secret power, all divinity. No enumeration could exhaust this infinitely complex idea. It is not a definite or definable power, it is Power itself in an absolute sense, with no epithet or determination of any sort. The various divine powers are only particular manifestations and personifications of it: each of them is this power seen under one of its numerous aspects" (p. 36). *Ashe*, for Verger, is a "non-anthropomorphic form of theism" (p. 38).

8. The invocations of the heads of ancestors are called *orikis*. Examples can be found in Chief J. A. Ayorinde, "Oriki," in *Sources of Yoruba History*, pp. 63–76. See also S. A. O. Babalola, *The Content and Form of Yoruba Ijala* (Oxford: Clarendon, 1966).

9. Ulli Beier devotes a richly illustrated volume to the state crowns of one Yoruba city (*Yoruba Beaded Crowns: Sacred Regalia of the Olokuku of Okuku* [London: Ethnographica, 1982]). This work is especially informative not only for its many photographs but also for its descriptions of the uses of the crown in royal rituals. It also contains examples of *orikis* for the crowns. For a fine exegesis of crown symbolism, see Robert Farris Thompson, "The Sign of the Divine King: Yoruba Bead-embroidered Crowns with Veil and Bird Decorations," in *African Art and Leadership*, edited by Douglas Fraser and Herbert Cole (Madison: University of Wisconsin Press, 1972).

10. For a basic overview of the varieties of Egungun, see William R. Bascom, *The Yoruba of Southwestern Nigeria* (New York: Holt, Rinehart & Winston, 1969), pp. 93–95. Again, art historian Robert Farris Thompson

offers an excellent analysis of the power and mystery of Egungun in *African Art in Motion: Icon and Act* (Berkeley: University of California Press, 1974), pp. 219–26. The glossy periodical *African Arts* devoted a special issue (vol. 11, no. 3 [April 1978]) to Egungun in which John Pemberton III, "Egungun Masquerades of the Igbomina Yoruba" (*African Arts*, vol. 11, no. 3 [April 1978]), is particularly helpful. For an early account of Egungun by a Yoruba scholar, see Isaac O. Delano, *The Soul of Nigeria* (London: T. Werner Laurie, 1937). Ulli Beier explains the presence of the ancestors in Egungun as a possession trance, such as that of *orisha* mediumship, in which the dancer is no longer himself but a vehicle for the archetypal ancestor whom he incarnates ("The Egungun Cult," *Nigeria* 51 [1956]: 385).

11. Pemberton, "Egungun Masquerades," p. 43.

12. Ibid., p. 41.

13. The Yoruba scholar and *babalawo* Wande Abimbola writes of the centrality of the idea of the "head" in Yoruba religion in "The Yoruba Concept of Human Personality," in *La notion de personne en Afrique noire* (Paris: Centre National de la Recherche Scientifique, 1973). In another work, Abimbola recounts an Ifa verse about *ori* that has great relevance for the Yoruba abroad. Ifa asks, "Who among the gods can accompany his devotee on a distant journey over the seas without turning back?" All the *orishas* attempt to show that they can cross the seas, but Ifa answers, "It is *ori* alone" (Wande Abimbola, *Ifa: An Exposition of Ifa Literary Corpus* [Ibadan: Oxford University Press Nigeria, 1976], pp. 137–42).

14. Wande Abimbola, "Iwa Pele: The Concept of Good Character in Ifa Literary Corpus," in *Yoruba Oral Tradition: Poetry in Music, Dance and Drama*, edited by Wande Abimbola (Ife: University of Ife Press, 1975), p. 395.

15. Abimbola, *Ifa*, p. 142.

16. On the connection of *ori* and Egungun, the Yoruba art historian Babatunde Lawal writes, "A typical Yoruba extended family comprises not only the living members but also the departed ones. To the Yoruba, the Dead are not dead, but will soon be back either as grandchildren or as Egungun" ("The Living Dead: Art and Immortality among the Yoruba of Nigeria," *Africa* 47, no. 1 [1977]: 59).

17. For descriptions of the character and qualities of the *orishas*, see Judith Gleason, *Orisha: The Gods of Yorubaland* (New York: Atheneum, 1971);

and Robert Farris Thompson, *Flash of the Spirit: African and Afro-American Art and Philosophy* (New York: Random House, 1983), pp. 1–99. Pierre Verger provides invaluable texts of *orikis* for the *orishas* in his *Notes sur le culte des orisa et vodun: à Bahia, la baie de tous les saints, au Brésil et à l'ancienne côte des esclaves en Afrique* (Dakar: L'Institut Français d'Afrique Noire, 1957). For collections of Yoruba myths about the *orishas* retold by accomplished fieldworkers, see Ulli Beier, *Yoruba Myths* (Cambridge: Cambridge University Press, 1980); and Harold Courlander, *Tales of Yoruba Gods and Heroes* (Greenwich, Conn.: Fawcett, 1973). For a treatment of the symbolic structural relationships among the *orishas*, see John Pemberton III, "A Cluster of Sacred Symbols: Orisa Worship among the Igbomina Yoruba of Ila-Orangun," *History of Religions*, vol. 17, no. 1 (August 1977).

Theologically minded scholars have been trying to define the divine status of the *orishas* with the same enthusiasm and inconclusiveness that has been applied to similar questions surrounding Jesus of Nazareth. Several Western interpreters of African religions have come to recognize this parallel as an ulterior motive through the work of the Ugandan poet and scholar Okot p'Bitek, who argues that "Western scholars have never been genuinely interested in African religions *per se*. Their works have all been part and parcel of some controversy or debate in the Western world" (*African Religions and Western Scholarship* [Nairobi: East African Publishing House, 1970], p. viii, quoted and critiqued in Benjamin Ray, *African Religions: Symbol, Ritual, and Community* [Englewood Cliffs, N.J.: Prentice-Hall, 1976], pp. 15–16; see also Newell S. Booth, "God and the Gods in West Africa," in *African Religions: A Symposium*, edited by Newell S. Booth [New York: NOK, 1977]).

18. Yoruba testimony is ambiguous about the origins of the *orishas* themselves. Ulli Beier argues that the *orishas* were formerly human beings who ascended to divine status. He recognizes a classic heroic pattern in this process wherein the *orisha* does great deeds, oversteps his authority, undergoes voluntary death, and experiences apotheosis. For an all-too-brief discussion of this pattern, see Beier, *Yoruba Myths*, pp. 69–70. In another work, Beier writes, "These stories all describe human beings who have widened the limits of human consciousness to such an extent that they can pass into the divine state." (*The Return of the Gods* [Cambridge: Cambridge University Press, 1975], p. 39).

19. For a scholarly proposal for the timeliness of Ogun worship, see Sandra Barnes, *Ogun: An Old God for a New Age*, Occasional Papers in Social Change, no. 3 (Philadelphia: Institute for the Study of Human Issues, 1980).

20. Ulli Beier, *Yoruba Poetry* (Cambridge: Cambridge University Press, 1970), p. 33. Reprinted with permission.

21. For an evocation of Oshun in the Old and New Worlds, see Joseph M. Murphy, "Oshun the Dancer," in *The Book of the Goddess Past and Present*, edited by Carl Olsen (New York: Crossroad, 1983), pp. 190–201.

22. Beier, *Yoruba Poetry*, p. 33.

23. On shrines, see Geoffrey Parrinder, *West African Religion*, 2d ed. (London: Epworth, 1961), pp. 60–74. Specific shrines are covered in more detail in Geoffrey Parrinder, *Religion in an African City* (London: Oxford University Press, 1953). For a discussion and map of Oyo shrines, see Peter Morton-Williams, "An Outline of the Cosmology and the Cult Organization of the Oyo Yoruba," *Africa*, vol. 34, no. 3 (1964).

24. The ethnographer of the Akan, Eva Meyerowitz, describes her visit to a Shango shrine in "Notes on the King-God Shango and His Temple at Ibadan, Southern Nigeria," *Man*, vol. 46, no. 27 (1946). A great deal of Shango's shrine symbolism is explored by a focus on the leather bags of Shango priests (see Joan Wescott and Peter Morton-Williams, "The Symbolism and Ritual Context of the Yoruba 'Laba Shango,' " *Journal of the Royal Anthropological Institute* 92, no. 1 [1962]). For an authoritative discussion of Shango shrines, sculpture, and symbolism, see Babatunde Lawal, *Yoruba Sango Sculpture in Historical Retrospect* (Ph.D. diss., Indiana University, 1970).

25. Beier, *Yoruba Poetry*, p. 31.

26. The faculties of Yoruba priesthood are best summarized by Ulli Beier, who derives three meanings from the Yoruba word *olorisha*. First, an *olorisha* is one who "has" an *orisha* in that he or she inherits the cultic obligations of an *orisha* or belongs to a certain lineage that supplies the *orisha's* priests. Second, an *olorisha* "*makes*" an *orisha* by making the songs, dances, and emblems that cause the *orisha* to be symbolically present. Third, an *olorisha* is one who "is" an *orisha* by becoming a medium for an *orisha* in ceremonial spirit possession (Beier, *The Return of the Gods*, p. 44).

William R. Bascom writes that Yoruba men and women become devotees of the *orishas* either by inheriting the *orisha's* worship from family elders or by being "called" to an *orisha's* service by outstanding events in their lives that are divined to be calls, especially the "call" of spirit possession ("The Sociological Role of the Yoruba Cult Group," *Memoirs of the American Anthropological Association*, no. 63 [1944]). Geoffrey Parrinder describes a distinction between the "true priests [who are] the sacrificers and leaders of the cultus, and the subordinate ranks of devotees, acolytes, servants and mediums or 'wives' of a god. The priest is the 'owner' of the god or his cultus (*olorisha, vodunon*);

the devotee or medium is the 'wife' (*iya-orisha*, *vodu-si*)" (*West African Religion*, p. 76). E. B. Idowu writes of Yoruba priesthood, "A devotee is an *olorisha*—"one who possesses *orisha*"; i.e., there is something of the divinity in him and it belongs to his position not only that he should offer worship to the *orisha* but also that he should absorb the *orisha* into his personality and manifest him" (*Olodumare*, p. 130).

On the reciprocal relationship between human beings and *orishas*, see Karen Barber, "How Man Makes God in West Africa: Yoruba Attitudes towards the *Orisa*," *Africa*, vol. 51, no. 3 (1981). For an illuminating perspective from a European-born *olorisha*, see Susanne Wenger and Gert Chesi, *A Life with the Gods in their Yoruba Homeland* (Worgl, Austria: Perlinger, 1983). Wenger's understanding of Yoruba religion is eclectic, but it may be the most profound of any yet written. For an in-depth description of initiation ceremonies for spirit mediumship in Brazil and Dahomey with extended quotes from earlier scholarship, see Verger, *Notes*, pp. 79–108.

27. For discussions of African dance, see Peggy Harper, "Dance in Nigeria," *Ethnomusicology*, vol. 13 (May 1969); and Robert Farris Thompson, "An Aesthetic of the Cool: West African Dance," *African Forum*, vol. 2, no. 2 (Fall 1966). See also William John Hanna and Judith Lynne Hanna, "The Social Significance of Dance in Black Africa," *Civilisations*, vol. 21, nos. 2–3 (1971). For an excellent description and analysis of Yoruba dances of spirit possession, see Margaret Thompson Drewal, "Symbols of Possession: A Study of Movement and Regalia in an Anago-Yoruba Ceremony," *Dance Research Journal*, vol. 7, no. 2 (1975).

28. See Pierre Verger, "Trance States in Orisha Worship," *Odu*, vol. 9 (September 1963). Verger offers a detailed description of a trance ceremony for Ogun in "Trance and Convention in Nago-Yoruba Spirit Mediumship," in *Spirit Mediumship and Society in Africa*, edited by John Beattie and John Middleton (New York: Africana, 1969).

29. While students of religion tend to see Yoruba initiates as priests, they must be understood to be doctors as well. Every *olorisha* is a herbalist and, until recently, the primary health care giver in Yorubaland. There is a growing interest in African traditional medicine and an increased willingness by Western-trained physicians to cooperate with traditional healers in therapy. For a report on such a project in one Yoruba city, see George E. Simpson, *Yoruba Religion and Medicine in Ibadan* (Ibadan: Ibadan University Press, 1980). See also Raymond Prince, "Indigenous Yoruba Psychiatry," in *Magic, Faith and Healing*, edited by Ari Kiev (New York: Free Press/Macmillan, 1964); Alexander Leighton et al., *Psychiatric Disorders among the Yoruba* (Ithaca, N.Y.: Cornell University Press, 1963); and Una Maclean, *Magical Medicine: A Nigerian Case Study* (Baltimore: Penguin, 1971). For details of Yoruba disease clas-

sification and herbal treatment, see Z. A. Ademuwagun et al., *African Therapeutic Systems* (Los Angeles: Crossroads, 1979); and Anthony D. Buckley, *Yoruba Medicine* (Oxford: Clarendon, 1985). Especially interesting in this regard is Pierre Verger's *Awon Ewe Osanyin: Yoruba Medicinal Leaves* (Ife: University of Ife Press, n.d.), which contains, in Yoruba and in English, the names, uses, and incantations associated with nearly two hundred plants.

30. Idowu, *Olodumare*, p. 73.

31. Beier, *Yoruba Poetry*, p. 27.

32. This well-known story is the subject for an important modern Yoruba drama (see Obotunde Ijimere, *The Imprisonment of Obatala* [London: Heinemann, 1966]). For another acclaimed drama based on *orisha* mythology, see Duro Lapido, *Three Yoruba Plays* (London: Heinemann, 1973), esp. "Oba Koso," the tragedy of Shango. The Yoruba laureate Wole Soyinka writes of the connections between ritual and theater in his essay "The Fourth Stage: Through the Mysteries of Ogun to the Origin of Yoruba Tragedy," in *Myth, Literature and the African World* (Cambridge: Cambridge University Press, 1976). This volume also contains critical essays on the works of Ijimere, Lapido, and other African writers.

33. The fullest treatment of the varieties and context of Yoruba sacrifice is J. Omosade Awolalu, *Yoruba Beliefs and Sacrificial Rites* (London: Longmans, 1979).

34. Idowu, *Olodumare*, 63.

35. There is a good deal of literature on Ifa divination, of which six full-length treatments should be noted. The earliest and most complete is Bernard Maupoil, *La géomancie à l'ancienne côte des esclaves*, Travaux et Mémoires, no. 42 (1943; reprint, Paris: L'Institut d'Ethnologie, 1961). The foremost American anthropologist of the Yoruba, William R. Bascom, produced a large catalog of Ifa verses in *Ifa Divination: Communication between Gods and Men in West Africa* (Bloomington: Indiana University Press, 1969). In addition to the verses are an extended introduction to Ifa, a short review of previous studies, and a large bibliography.

Bascom sees Ifa as a kind of therapy, its healing power lying in the interpretation of its cryptic messages through a process of consultation between a client and a professional diagnostician. The Yoruba scholar Wande Abimbola, himself a trained *babalawo*, has consistently interpreted Ifa as literature rather than therapy. He has produced a number of articles and books on Ifa, notably *Ifa*, and esp. *Ifa Divination Poetry* (New York: NOK, 1977). For Abimbola, it is the rich enigmatic and allusive poetry that gives Ifa its efficacy.

Even to speakers of Yoruba, Ifa can be obscure, and it can present difficult interpretive problems to non-Yoruba. Judith Gleason has created an imaginative interpretation of the first sixteen *odu* of Ifa in her *A Recitation of Ifa: Oracle of the Yoruba* (New York: Grossman, 1973). The most recent full-length work on Ifa is E. M. McClelland, *The Cult of Ifa among the Yoruba* (London: Ethnographica, 1982). This book provides invaluable information on the training and initiation rites of Ifa priests and the connections between Ifa and medicine.

Among shorter pieces on Ifa, Raymond H. Prince has written a lucid, short study of Ifa and the connection between divination and sacrifice in the pamphlet *Ifa: Yoruba Divination and Sacrifice* (Ibadan: Ibadan University Press, 1966). For a perspective on African divination as a distinctly religious phenomenon, see Evan M. Zeuss, "Divination and Deity in African Religions," *History of Religions*, vol. 15, no. 2 (November 1975). For an essay on the symbolism of Ifa divination instruments filled with details of exegesis by *babalawos*, see Rowland Abiodun, "Ifa Art Objects," in *Yoruba Oral Tradition*. For an account of a particular family of diviners and an exposition of their shrine, see Margaret Thompson Drewal and Henry John Drewal, "An Ifa Diviner's Shrine in Ijebuland," *African Arts*, vol. 16, no. 2 (1983). The issue of *African Arts* in which this article appears is a memorial edition for William Bascom and contains a number of articles of interest to scholars of the Yoruba.

36. Abimbola, *Ifa*, p. 44.

37. McClelland, *The Cult of Ifa among the Yoruba*, p. 88.

38. See William Fagg, John Pemberton, and Bryce Holcomb, *Yoruba Beadwork: Art of Nigeria* (New York: Rizzoli, 1980).

39. Abimbola, *Ifa Divination Poetry*, p. 49.

40. My suggestions for the interpretation of this *odu* follow Bascom's model of the Ifa process. While my interpretaton is only hypothetical, I am assured by my friend *babalawo* Ifayemi Elebu-ibon of Oshogbo that it is a reasonable one.

2: CUBA

1. For the history of the fall of Oyo and the slave wars of the nineteenth century see the works cited in n. 3 of chap. 1 above. For general histories of this period, see J. D. Fage, *An Introduction to the History of West Africa* (Cambridge: Cambridge University Press, 1961); Obaro Ikime, *The Groundwork of Nigerian History* (Lagos: Heinemann, 1980); J. F. A. Ajayi and M. Crowder, eds., *History of West Africa*, 3d ed. (New York: Columbia University Press, 1985); and Adu A. Boahen, ed., *Topics in West African History* (London: Longmans, 1986).

2. Thomas J. Bowen, *Adventures and Missionary Labors in Several Countries in the Interior of Africa from 1849–1856* (1857; reprint, London: Frank Cass, 1968), p. 113.

3. For a popular history of Cuba that stresses this eighteenth-century transformation, see Hugh Thomas, *Cuba: The Pursuit of Freedom* (New York: Harper & Row, 1971). This is a massive work, but it is readable throughout. Although the stress is on the revolution of 1959, it recognizes and documents the Afro-Cuban contributions to Cuban history and culture.

4. See Joseph E. Harris, *Africa and Africans as Seen by Classical Writers: The William Leo Hansberry African History Notebook* (Washington: Howard University Press, 1977), vol. 2. See also Jean Vercouter et al., *The Image of the Black in Western Art* (Cambridge, Mass.: Harvard University Press, 1976). For challenging works on the African influences on European culture, see Cheikh Anta Diop, *The African Origin of Civilization: Myth or Reality* (Westport, Conn.: Lawrence Hill, 1974); and Ivan Van Sertima, *African Presence in Early Europe* (New Brunswick, N.J.: Transaction, 1985). Van Sertima is best known for his work on the African presence in the Americas, *They Came before Columbus* (New York: Random House, 1977).

5. Herbert S. Klein, *Slavery in the Americas* (Chicago: University of Chicago Press, 1967), pp. 65–66. See also Arthur F. Corwin, *Spain and the Abolition of Slavery in Cuba: 1817–1886* (Austin: University of Texas Press, 1967), p. 5.

6. Klein, *Slavery in the Americas*, pp. 135–36.

7. Bartolome Las Casas, *The Devastation of the Indies: A Brief Account* (1552; reprint, New York: Seabury, 1974). Las Casas's vivid descriptions of Spanish brutality served as effective propaganda for Spain's rivals in the New World, and they fostered the *leyenda negra* to depict the Conquest as an unending series of Spanish atrocities. For insight on

the *leyenda negra*, see Charles Gibson, *Spain in America* (New York: Harper & Row, 1966). For correctives, see Silvio A. Zavala, *New Viewpoints on the Spanish Colonization of America* (Philadelphia: University of Pennsylvania Press, 1943); and Lewis Hanke, *The Spanish Struggle for Justice in the Conquest of America* (Philadelphia: University of Pennsylvania Press, 1949).

8. The definitive account of these numbers is Philip D. Curtin, *The Atlantic Slave Trade: A Census* (Madison: University of Wisconsin Press, 1969). See also Basil Davidson, *Black Mother: The Years of the African Slave Trade* (Boston: Little, Brown, 1961); and Herbert S. Klein, *The Middle Passage* (Princeton, N.J.: Princeton University Press, 1978).

9. Stanley M. Elkins, *Slavery: A Problem in American Institutional and Intellectual Life* (New York: Grosset, 1963), p. 98.

10. Hubert H. S. Aimes, *A History of Slavery in Cuba: 1511–1868* (1907; reprint, New York: Octagon, 1967), p. 269.

11. Curtin, *The Atlantic Slave Trade*, p. 46.

12. See Fernando Ortiz, *Hampa afro-cubana: los negros esclavos* (Havana: Revista Bimestre Cubana, 1916), and *Cuban Counterpoint* (New York: Knopf, 1949). On the economics of the sugar industry, see Ramiro Guerra y Sánchez, *Sugar and Society in the Caribbean* (New Haven, Conn.: Yale University Press, 1964). For a comprehensive account of life in the sugar mills, see Manuel Moreno Fraginals, *The Sugarmill* (New York: Monthly Review Press, 1976). For sociological analyses of Cuban sugar society, see Franklin W. Knight, *Slave Society in Cuba during the Nineteenth Century* (Madison: University of Wisconsin Press, 1970); and Gwendolyn Mildo Hall, *Social Control in Slave Plantation Societies* (Baltimore: Johns Hopkins University Press, 1971).

13. Knight, *Slave Society in Cuba*, p. 59. See also Juan Francisco Manzano, *The Life and Poems of a Cuban Slave*, edited by Edward J. Mullen (Hamden, Conn.: Archon, 1981).

14. C. Stanley Urban, "The Africanization of Cuba Scare, 1853–1855," *Hispanic American Historical Review*, vol. 37 (1957).

15. Ortiz, *Hampa afro-cubana*, pp. 430–31.

16. Esteban Montejo, *Autobiography of a Runaway Slave* (New York: Pantheon, 1968), p. 26. Montejo is quoted on this subject in chap. 11 below.

17. Montejo, *Autobiography*, pp. 43–44.

18. José L. Franco, "Maroons and Slave Rebellions in the Spanish Territories," in *Maroon Societies: Rebel Slave Communities in the Americas*, edited by Richard Price (Garden City, N.Y.: Anchor/Doubleday, 1973). See also Francisco Pérez de la Riva, "Cuban Palenques," in ibid.

19. See Knight, *Slave Society in Cuba*, p. 60; and Klein, *Slavery in the Americas*, p. 164.

20. See Ortiz, *Hampa afro-cubana*, p. 312; and Klein, *Slavery in the Americas*, pp. 146–47.

21. As Roger Bastide reminds us, the designation of race reflects culture as much as biology. He writes, "Every nation has its own racial ideology and the census rolls will tend to express this ideological pattern rather than hard demographic facts" (*African Civilisations in the New World* [New York: Harper & Row, 1972], p. 15). For census figures, see Ortiz, *Hampa afro-cubana*, pp. 22–23. See also Kenneth F. Kiple, *Blacks in Colonial Cuba, 1774–1899* (Gainesville: University of Florida Press, 1976). For a hemispheric perspective on *gente de color* with an article on Cuba by Franklin Knight, see David W. Cohen and Jack P. Greene, *Neither Slave nor Free* (Baltimore: Johns Hopkins University Press, 1972).

22. Klein, *Slavery in the Americas*, pp. 202, 236.

23. William R. Bascom, *Shango in the New World* (Austin: University of Texas, African and Afro-American Research Institute, 1972).

24. Herbert S. Klein, "Anglicanism, Catholicism and the Negro Slave," *Comparative Studies in Society and History*, vol. 8 (1965–66): 300.

25. Klein, *Slavery in the Americas*, p. 80.

26. See Alonzo de Sandoval, *De instauranda aethiopum salute* (1627; reprint, Bogota: Empresa Nacional de Publicaciones, 1956). This remarkable work of 600 pages contains a detailed summary of contemporary knowledge of African customs. Most important is its third section, which details the catechetical procedure that Sandoval and his student Claver carried out on the docks of Cartagena. For an uncritical survey of the work of Claver and others, see Edward D. Reynolds, *Jesuits for the Negro* (New York: America Press, 1949).

27. See Augustin Roman, "The Popular Piety of the Cuban People" (M. A. thesis, Barry College, 1976), p. 16; and Moreno, *The Sugarmill*, p. 58.

28. See Ortiz, *Cuban Counterpoint*, pp. 98–100.

29. See Fernando Ortiz, *Los cabildos africanos* (Havana: La Universal, 1921).

30. Ibid., p. 18.

31. Ibid., p. 24.

32. Perhaps as early as 1839, then, we find a Lucumi symbolic correspondence between Shango and Saint Barbara.

33. Ortiz, *Los cabildos africanos*, p. 24. This identity between drum and dance is recognized throughout West Africa and persists in the names of santería ceremonies such as *bembe* and the more general Spanish word used by *santeros, tambor*.

34. See Fernando Ortiz, *La fiesta afrocubana del "día de reyes"* (Havana: Imprenta El Siglo XX, 1925).

35. Ortiz, *La fiesta afrocubana*, p. 6.

36. See Lydia Cabrera, *La sociedad secreta Abakuá* (Miami: Ediciónes Universal, 1970); and Robert Farris Thompson, *Flash of the Spirit*, pp. 224–68.

37. See Lydia Cabrera, *Reglas de Congo: Palo Monte—Mayombe* (Miami: Ediciónes Universal, 1979).

38. Montejo, *Autobiography*, pp. 33–35.

39. It is also called *la regla lucumi* or, simply, Lucumi or Ocha.

40. Cabrera, *La sociedad secreta Abakuá*, p. 9.

41. Montejo, *Autobiography*, p. 169. Thompson has shown that the Efik leopard societies had jural functions, and so it may come to light that Cuban Abakuá violence was a sanctioned means of social control. For an exciting story of the social role of secret societies in Haiti, see Wade

Davis, *The Serpent and the Rainbow* (New York: Simon & Schuster, 1985).

42. See G. R. Coulthard, *Race and Colour in Caribbean Literature* (London: Oxford University Press, 1962); and Roberto Gonzáles Echevarría, *Alejo Carpentier: The Pilgrim at Home* (Ithaca, N.Y.: Cornell University Press, 1977). See also Ramon Guirao, *Orbita de la poesía afrocubana* (Havana, 1939); and Jorge Luis Morales, *Poesía afroantillana y negrista* (Rio Pedras: Editorial Universitaria de Puerto Rico, 1976). For a collection of critical essays by Cuban scholars, see Oscar Fernández de la Vega and Alberto N. Pamiés, eds., *Iniciacion a la poesía afro-americana* (Miami: Ediciónes Universal, 1973). For a survey of Afro-Cuban poetry and prose, see Enrique Noble, ed., *Literatura afro-hispanoamericana* (Leighton, Mass.: Xerox College Publishing, 1973).

3: BOTÁNICA

1. For the story of Caridad's appearance and the devotion of the Cuban people to her, see Irene Wright, "Nuestra Señora de la Caridad del Cobré," *Hispanic American Historical Review*, vol. 5, no. 4 (1922); and Ruben Vargas Ugarte, *Historia del culto de Maria en Ibero-America* (Madrid: Talleres Graficos Jura, 1956).

2. Following Melville Herskovits, nearly every treatment of Afro-Latin religions has included a chart depicting correspondences between African spirits and Catholic saints. Herskovits thought these religions were case studies of cultural "syncretism." I will have a good deal to say about "syncretism" and santería in chap. 11 below. For a pioneer study of *orisha*-saint correspondences, see Melville Herskovits, "African Gods and Catholic Saints in New World Negro Belief," *American Anthropologist*, vol. 39 (1937).

The organization of this chart is most indebted to Maya Deren's classification of the Vodun *loa* (see *Divine Horsemen: The Living Gods of Haiti* [New York: Thames & Hudson, 1953]), pp. 82–83).

3. An excellent summary of santería ritual centering on sacrifice to the *orisha* stones is William R. Bascom, "The Focus of Cuban *Santería*," *Southwestern Journal of Anthropology*, vol. 1, no. 1 (1950).

4. This view of Eleggua is drawn from Robert Farris Thompson, *Flash of the Spirit*, pp. 18–33. For a study of Eleggua as a trickster compared with other African tricksters, see Robert D. Pelton, *The Trickster in*

West Africa: A Study of Mythic Irony and Sacred Delight (Berkeley and Los Angeles: University of California Press, 1980).

5. Idowu—a "Western-minded Yoruba," in Thompson's phrase—suggests this parallel (*Olodumare*, p. 80).

6. In her great work *El monte* (Miami: Ediciónes Universal, 1975), Lydia Cabrera documents over 550 herbs and plants in use in santería ceremonies and cures. These are cataloged with their Spanish, Latin, and Lucumi names, their patron *orishas*, and their ritual and medicinal uses. See also George E. Brandon, "*The Dead Sell Memories: An Anthropological Study of Santería in New York City*" (Ph.D. diss., Rutgers University, 1983), pp. 322–32, 566–71, which has the most complete description of santería rites in English.

7. Again, Thompson is our guide through the symbolism of Osanyin; see his *Flash of the Spirit*, pp. 42–51, and "Icons of the Mind: Yoruba Herbalism Art in Atlantic Perspective," *African Arts*, vol. 8, no. 3 (1975). An exemplary collection of prayer texts for Osanyin has been assembled by American *babalorisha* John Mason (*Osanyin* [New York: Yoruba Theological Archministry, 1983]).

8. See Thompson, *Flash of the Spirit*, pp. 45–51. A variety of *osun* styles are described and commented on in Geraldine Torres Guerra, "Un elemento ritual: el 'osun,' " *Etnologia y folklore*, vol. 3 (January–June 1967).

9. It might well be argued that santería is, in essence, herbalism since the herbs and the *orishas* are fundamentally expressions of the same force. Senior *santeros* told Lydia Cabrera, "No hay santo sin *ewe*" (There is no saint without herbs).

10. Allan Kardec, *The Spirit's Book* (Sao Paulo: Livraria Allan Kardec Editora, n.d.). There are many editions and translations of Kardec's books. Mine is published by a Kardec society in Brazil and claims to be the first English translation.

11. There is a good deal of writing about Puerto Rican spiritualism, most of it from the point of view of psychiatrists and psychiatric social workers who see it as an alternative form of healing. For an inauspiciously titled but excellent study from this perspective, see Alan Harwood, *Rx: Spiritist as Needed* (New York: Wiley, 1977), which has an extensive bibliography. In the same series is Vincent Crapanzano and Vivian Garrison, eds., *Case Studies in Spirit Possession* (New York: Wiley, 1977). For a well-written description of a spiritualist ceremony, see Dan Wakefield, *Island in the City* (Boston: Houghton, Mifflin, 1959).

4: ILE

1. I am indebted to Steve Quintana III for some of the facts of Padrino and Obashalewa's biographies.

2. For a description of this display and many other aspects of the tradition, especially the *bembe*, see Judith Gleason, *Santeria, Bronx* (New York: Atheneum, 1975). This book is a novel by an experienced fieldworker and an important influence on my own understanding of the religion.

3. For a remarkably compact description of the objects in home shrines, see Lydia González Huguet, "La casa-templo en la regla de ocha," *Etnologia y folklore*, vol. 5 (January–June 1968). See also Oscar Lewis et al., *Four Men: Living the Revolution: An Oral History of Contemporary Cuba* (Urbana: University of Illinois Press, 1977). This book contains autobiographical sketches of four Cubans, one of whom, Lázaro Benedí Rodríguez, is both a *santero* and a Communist party official. In discussing his life, he offers a great deal of information about the world of Afro-Cuban religions. His stories are full of gentle humor, and his wife tells us that he used to let their children play with the sacred stones and objects in his shrine room.

5: IFA

1. A superb source on the rites of initiation of the *babalawo* priesthood is Lourdes López, *Estudio de un babalao* (Havana: Universidad de Havana, Departamento de Actividades Culturales, 1978).

2. For scholarly work on Cuban divination by an accomplished anthropologist of the Yoruba, see William R. Bascom, "Two Forms of Afro-Cuban Divination," in *Acculturation in the Americas*, edited by Sol Tax (Chicago: University of Chicago Press, 1952). In the introduction to his book on cowrie shell divination, Bascom tells us a great deal about divination in Cuba (see *Sixteen Cowries: Yoruba Divination from Africa to the New World* [Bloomington: Indiana University Press, 1980]).

3. Ifayemi Elebu-ibon tells me that the stone indicates the good fortune of a long life, the bone the bad fortune of death, and the shell the good fortune of wealth.

4. These *odu* are not the ones that fell on that day.

5. Bascom estimated that there were some two hundred *babalawos* in Havana in the late 1940s (see "Two Forms of Afro-Cuban Divination," p. 171). Oscar Lewis quotes an estimate of three hundred in all of

Cuba in the 1960s (*Four Men,* p. 72n). The Puerto Rican ethnomusicologist Hector Vega told me in 1981 that there were 265 *babalawos* in Cuba at that time. Bascom was told in the late 1960s that there were eighty-three *babalawos* living in Miami (see *Shango in the New World*). I am guessing that there are no more than ten or fifteen true *babalawos* in New York in the 1980s. I base this guess on Padrino's assertion that it is impossible to "make Ifa" in the United States because the spiritual ingredients and experience necessary for the initiation are unavailable here. For Padrino, anyone claiming to be a *babalawo* "made" in the United States is an imposter.

6. Any story from the Ifa oracle is a *pataki,* and most experienced *santeros* know hundreds of them. A *babalawo* might know thousands. For a large collection of *patakis* edited by a Cuban-American believer, see Julio Garcia-Cortez, *Pataki: leyendas y misterios de los orishas africanos* (Miami: Ediciónes Universal, 1980). For a systematic presentation by a scholar, see Mercedes Cros Sandoval, *La religión afrocubana* (Madrid: Playor, 1975). For English retellings of some *patakis,* see Migene González-Wippler, *Tales of the Orishas* (New York: Original Publications, 1985).

6: WARRIORS

1. The Drewals report that, in Yorubaland, the *osun* is likened to a tree, and so it may be that Padrino's phrase refers to his "transplanting" of my life by his fabrication of my *osun* (see Drewal and Drewal, "An Ifa Diviner's Shrine in Ijebuland," pp. 65–66). This article also sheds light on the symbolism of the cock atop the *osun* by relating a story that Ifa defeats Death by plucking a cock and offering it to Death. The Drewals say that the *osun* is the babalawo's "weapon against death" (p. 65).

2. Many Yoruba myths tell of the symbiotic relationship between the diviner and the herbalist. On the friendship of Orunmila and Osanyin, see Beier, *Yoruba Myths,* pp. 54–55.

3. Thompson sees Eshu's knife as an allusion to the trickster's outrageous phallicism. He translates an Afro-Cuban song to Eleggua in this way:

> Pointed-knife (Penis), Pointed-Knife of the Wonder-Worker
> No-Load-Upon-Your-Head, Pointed-Knife, Wonder-Worker
> No-Load-Upon-Upon-Head, Your Majesty
> Man-With-Pointed-Knife-Springing-From-Your-Head

> (Thompson, *Black Gods and Kings,* p. 4/2)

Herskovits, in the liner notes for *Afro-Bahian Religious Songs* (Washington, D.C.: Library of Congress, 1947), translated the words to a song for Eshu that is also well known in santería:

> *Eshu tiriri*
> *Bara abebe*
> *Tiriri lona*

> Eshu, the Awesome
> O powerful knife
> The Awesome one, on the road.

4. Cabrera, *El monte*, p. 381.

5. I have been able to transcribe and translate this song that Padrino taught me by means of John Mason's work in *Osanyin* (p. 5):

> *Osun Bori Bo Ma Du Bule*
> *Duro Gangan La A Bo'sun Awo*
> *Lakan Laka La A Bo'sun Awo*

> Osun be the conquerer do not sleep
> We always find the staff of the initiate standing firm
> We always find the staff of the initiate jumping on one foot.

6. The yellow and green beads, sacred to Ifa, may represent the colors of forest herbs, again reinforcing the connection between the *orisha* of wisdom and the *orisha* of leaves. Thompson records these words of a Nigerian *babalawo*: "Our priests of divination and herbalists went, at the beginning, to the god of divination. He gave them strands of alternating green and yellow beads saying, 'this is your sign.' These beads stand for Ewe Ifa, the leaf of divination" ("Icons of the Mind," p. 54).

7: ELEKES

1. Matanzas has a high reputation as a center for the conservation of African religions (see Lydia Cabrera, *Lalaguna sagrada de San Joaquín* [Madrid: Ediciónes R, 1973], which has many photographs of a lakeside ceremony to Yemaya in Matanzas.)

2. For a description of the preparation of *omiero*, see Lydia Cabrera, *Yemayá y Ochún* (Miami: Ediciónes Universal, 1980), pp. 156–58. In Africa, *omiero* is water to soften the hearts of the *orishas*, and it refers specifically to the fluid drawn from snails that is dear to Obatala (see R. C.

Abraham, *Dictionary of Modern Yoruba* [London: University of London Press, 1958], pp. 286, 474).

3. John Mason records and translates a *moyuba* similar to the one that I learned from Madrina (*Sin Egun* [New York: Yoruba Theological Archministry, 1981], pp. 9–10):

> Mo Juba Olofi
> Mo Juba Gbogbo Orisa
> Mo Juba Gbogbo Iyalosa, Babalosa, Oluo Ara Orun
> Mo Juba Gbogbo Egun
> Nbelese Olodumare Iba'iye Orun
> Mo Juba [names of family dead]

> I salute God
> I salute all Orishas
> I salute all mothers of Orishas, fathers of Orishas, elders who are in the heavens
> I salute all the ancestors that bow at the feet of God, chief of the heavenly world
> I salute [names of family dead]

4. For a number of prayer texts in Lucumi, Spanish, and English, see Brandon, "The Dead Sell Memories," pp. 200–222. See also a classification and analysis of santería prayers in Isabel Mercedes Castellanos, "The Use of Language in Afro-Cuban Religion" (Ph.D. diss., Georgetown University, 1976), pp. 102–13. For a discussion of the *caminos* of the *orishas*, see Nicolas V. Angarica, *Manual del orihate (religion Lucumi)* (Miami: Ediciónes Universal, 1979).

5. Lydia Cabrera writes of the love and responsibility between *iyalorishas* and their spiritual children in *Yemayá y Ochún*—esp. the chapter on *iyalorishas*, pp. 235–65.

8: ASIENTO

1. Each *ile* recognizes a different number of days in the *asiento* ceremonies for different *orishas*. The *asiento* ceremonies for Yemaya and Oshun are thoroughly described by Lydia Cabrera in *Yemayá y Ochún*. An excellent description of *asiento* as well as many other santería ceremonies can be found in Migene González-Wippler, *The Santeria Experience* (Englewood Cliffs, N.J.: Prentice-Hall, 1982). For a complete and careful record of *asiento* symbolism, see also Brandon, "The Dead Sell Memories." For a clear and systematic presentation of the ranks of the santería priesthood, see Julio Sanchez, *La religión de los orichas* (Hato Rey, P.R.: Coleccíon Estudios Afrocaribeños, 1978). This book is by

a trained anthropologist and is the best work on santería from that perspective. Isabel Castellanos focuses on the ritual functions of a little-noted aspect of *asiento* ceremonies, the ritual questions asked of the *iyawo* to bring him or her into the world of *santo* (see "The Use of Language in Afro-Cuban Religion," pp. 81–101).

2. Cabrera, *Yemayá y Ochún*, p. 129.

3. For an overview of *dilogun* divination and over seven hundred pages of Nigerian *dilogun* verses, see Bascom, *Sixteen Cowries*. Some detailed comparative material can be found in Bascom, "Two Forms of Afro-Cuban Divination." There are a number of books written to instruct believers in the arts of *dilogun* divination. The most concise presentation of the basics of *dilogun* is Lydia Cabrera's handbook, *Koeko iyawó: aprende novicia* (Miami: Ediciónes Universal, 1980). For a massive book of instruction, privately printed, see Enrique Cortés, *Manual del oriaté* (New York: Vilaragut Articulos Religiosos Corp., 1980). Another privately printed work (without publisher or date) that can be found in many *botánicas* is Carlos Elizondo, *Manual del italero de la religión Lucumí*. The best organized presentation by an *italero* is Andres R. Rogers, *Los caricoles: historia de sus letras* (Washington, D.C.: Libreria Latinoamericana, 1973).

4. For an outline of the regulations of the *iyawo's* novitiate, see Sanchez, *La religión de los orichas*, pp. 92–94.

9: BEMBE

1. Though there are some printed collections of *suyeres*, it is very difficult to find Spanish or English translations. Pierre Verger's *Notes* contains texts of prayers from both Nigeria and Brazil translated into French. John Mason's publications with the Yoruba Theological Archministry contain several santería texts rendered into standard Yoruba and given English translations. See also Brandon, "The Dead Sell Memories," pp. 458–66. Extensive transcriptions of Lucumi texts can be found in Lydia Cabrera, *Koeko iyawó*; and Miguel Ramos, *Ase Omo Osain . . . Ewe Aye* (Carolina, P.R.: 1982).

2. For a five-volume encyclopedic survey of Afro-Cuban musical instruments, see Fernando Ortiz, *Los instrumentos de la musica afrocubana* (Havana: Cardenas, 1952–55). For information on the *bata* orchestra, see 4: 205–321.

3. For an excellent study of santería drumming to which this chapter is much indebted, see Robert Alan Friedman, *Making an Abstract World Concrete* (Ann Arbor: University Microfilms, 1982).

4. I have also heard it said that Eleggua must be "sent away" so that he will not disturb the ceremony with disruptive tricks.

5. I am indebted to Adetokunbo Adekanmbi of Georgetown University for her work in translating these Lucumi songs.

6. In other parts of the Yoruba world, this liturgical order of call is called *shire*, but I was unable to confirm this word among Padrino's *ile*. This order of *orisha* invocation varies from *ile* to *ile*, and each is committed to the correctness of its order.

7. I believe that the *orishas* are better understood as rhythms than as personalities. From this perspective, we might say that it is not because Shango is aggressive that his rhythms are aggressive but rather that because the rhythms are aggressive Shango is aggressive.

8. Most of the *bembe* songs seem to be divisible into two parts. The first part is invocation, calling the *orisha* to come and join the proceedings. The second part is communion; the rhythms become more forceful, sustaining an altered state of consciousness both in the "horse" of the *orisha* and in the community in the *orisha*'s presence. For a musicological analysis of the transition between these states, see Morton Marks, "Uncovering Ritual Structures in Afro-American Music," in *Religious Movements in Contemporary America*, edited by Irving I. Zaretsky and Mark P. Leone (Princeton, N.J.: Princeton University Press, 1974).

9. For an excellent early description of a ceremonial appearance of Oshun in Cuba, see Irene Wright, *Cuba* (New York: Macmillan, 1910), pp. 147–48.

10. A similar thing happened to Migene González-Wippler in her description of a *bembe*, where the *orisha* revealed whose child she was (see *The Santeria Experience*, pp. 30–34). The best description of a *bembe* is still Gleason, *Santeria, Bronx*, pp. 97–112.

11. For a study of trance speech and behavior, see Castellanos, "The Use of Language in Afro-Cuban Religions," pp. 131–40.

12. I am uninterested in finding an "explanation" for this experience, other than to ground its meaning in the revelation of the divine. I know that I am influenced in its description by Maya Deren's writing of her "possession" in Haiti (see *Divine Horsemen*, pp. 247–62).

10: ETHNOHISTORY

1. Melville J. Herskovits, *The Myth of the Negro Past* (Boston: Beacon, 1958).

2. For a review of the work of Herskovits and the arguments of his critics, see the editors' introduction to Norman E. Whitten and John F. Szwed, eds., *Afro-American Anthropology: Contemporary Perspectives* (New York: Free Press/Macmillan, 1970), pp. 25–30. According to Whitten and Szwed, the primary argument against Herskovits is his emphasis on ritual and symbolism as a focus of culture and his neglect of social structure. This does not seem to tell very strongly against the usefulness of an ethnohistorical interpretation of santería. To be sure, santería is much more than isolated bundles of Africanisms and the way that santería expresses and creates alternative patterns of social organization can make an important study. For such a sociological interpretation of santería, see Ndeye Anna Fall, *La santeria dans la société cubaine* (Dakar: University of Dakar, 1975).

3. Herskovits, *The Myth of the Negro Past*, p. 8.

4. See William R. Bascom, "Urbanization among the Yoruba," *American Journal of Sociology*, vol. 60 (1955). On the antiquity of Yoruba civilization, see n. 1 in chap. 1 above.

5. Albert Raboteau speaks of the "death of the gods" on North American soil, but he provides some examples of Afro-American folklore that identify thunderstorms with axes (*Slave Religion: The "Invisible Institution" in the Antebellum South* [New York: Oxford University Press, 1978]). The Barbadian poet and critic Edward Kamau Brathwaite suggests that the hammer-wielding hero of American railroad folklore, John Henry, is none other than Shango in New World guise ("The African Presence in Caribbean Literature," in *Slavery, Colonialism, and Racism*, edited by Sidney W. Mintz [New York: Norton, 1974]).

6. Ortiz, *Hampa afro-cubana*, pp. 22–23.

7. Curtin, *The Atlantic Slave Trade*, pp. 246–47.

8. Bastide, *African Civilisations in the New World*, p. 11.

9. Klein, "Anglicanism, Catholicism and the Negro Slave," pp. 305–6.

10. Bastide, *African Civilisations in the New World.*

11. See Frank Tannenbaum, *Slave and Citizen: The Negro in the Americas* (New York: Knopf, 1946). Klein has argued for Tannenbaum's thesis that, even in the sugar mills, Spanish law offered some protection to the lives of the slaves and some mitigation of their suffering. Sidney Mintz writes, "When Cuba's slaveholders became politically powerful,

as plantation slavery became capitalistic in a fuller sense, they handily defeated the intent of the 1789 laws designed to ameliorate the slaves' condition, and that humanitarian tradition, universalistic religion and past practice did not prevent them from doing so" (*Caribbean Transformations* [Chicago: Aldine, 1974], pp. 71–72).

12. In 1856, Alexander Humbolt wrote, "These comparisons demonstrate a state of affairs in the latter island [Cuba] infinitely more favorable [than in Jamaica] to the physical preservation and manumission of the Negroes; but what a sorrowful spectacle is presented by Christian and civilized nations disputing which of the two, in three centuries, has destroyed the least number of Africans, by reducing them to slavery!" (*The Island of Cuba* [1856; reprint, New York: Negro Universities Press, 1969], p. 225).

13. See Michel Laguerre, "The Failure of Christianity among the Slaves of Haiti," *Freeing the Spirit*, vol. 2, no. 4 (1973). I do not wish to act as an apologist for the Catholic church, far less for slavery, but I would like to know what would constitute "success" in a religious mission. If successful Christianization means the achievement of a human society based on realized Christian principles of faith, hope, and love, a society in which people love their neighbors as themselves, then the church has never been successful in its two-thousand-year history. If success is constituted by the development of a Christian piety based on an accurate understanding of the church's dogmatic principles, then the church has failed its mission to the bulk of the people who profess Christianity. If success in Latin America is constituted by the eradication of all vestiges of African religious tradition, then, finally, the church did indeed fail.

14. Elsa Goveia, "Comment on 'Anglicanism, Catholicism and the Negro Slave,' " *Comparative Studies in Society and History* 8 (1965–66): 330.

15. Klein, *Slavery in the Americas*, p. 100.

16. Reynolds, *Jesuits for the Negro*, p. 22.

17. Ralph Korngold, *Citizen Toussaint* (New York: Macmillan, 1945), p. 39. I am indebted to my teacher Leonard E. Barrett for pointing out this quote to me. See his use of it in Leonard E. Barrett, "African Religions in the Americas," in *The Black Experience in Religion*, edited by C. Eric Lincoln (Garden City, N.Y.: Doubleday, 1974), p. 322.

18. Most New World missionals were concerned with the evangelization of the Indians, and it was to this project that the tremendous intellectual energies of the sixteenth century were dedicated (see Pedro

Borges, *Methodos misionales en la cristianización de America en el siglo XVI* [Madrid: Departmento de Misionologia Española, 1960]).

19. On the destruction of the Yoruba family cult, Bastide writes, "Slavery totally destroyed these *lignages*. Though the notion that one can "inherit the god"—on the distaff as well as the male side—still survives in America, the only true reality which has been preserved is, of necessity, that embodied in the fraternities. The family cult group has disappeared" (*African Civilisations in the New World*, p. 116). Later, Bastide puts the point more theoretically: "Slavery caused a breach between the superstructures and the infrastructures. . . . The African social structures were shattered, the values preserved. But these values could live only by creating for themselves new social frameworks, new institutions capable of perpetuating themselves and of being transmitted from one generation to the next. In brief, the superstructure had to secrete a· society" (Roger Bastide, *The African Religions of Brazil* [Baltimore: Johns Hopkins University Press, 1978], p. 56).

20. Ortiz, *Los cabildos afrocubanos.*

21. There is today a thriving devotion to the *egun* in Salvador da Bahia, Brazil, complete with the sumptuous appliquéd costumes of their Nigerian counterparts (see Juana Elbein Dos Santos and Deoscoredes M. Dos Santos, "Ancestor Worship in Bahia: The Egun-Cult," *Journal de la Société des Américanistes*, vol. 58 [1969]; and also Mikelle Smith Omari, *From the Inside to the Outside: The Art and Ritual of Bahian Candomble*, Museum of Cultural History, Monograph Series no. 24 [Los Angeles: University of California, Los Angeles, 1984]). On Egungun in Cuba, see Fernando Ortiz, *Los bailes y el teatro de los negros en el folklore de Cuba* (Havana: Ediciónes Cardenas, 1951), p. 349; and Miguel Ramos, *Oro . . . Egungun: Honras de Egungun* (Carolina, P.R.: 1982).

22. Bastide, *African Civilisations in the New World*, p. 116.

23. To account for differences between traditional forms and their meanings, Melville J. Herskovits uses the word "reinterpretation." He defines it in this way: "Reinterpretation . . . is the process by which old meanings are ascribed to new elements or by which new values change the cultural significance of old forms" (*Man and His Works* [New York: Knopf, 1948], p. 553).

24. R. Redfield, R. Linton, and M. Herskovits, "Memorandum for the Study of Acculturation," *American Anthropologist* 38 (1936): 149.

25. Ortiz, *Cuban Counterpoint*, p. 98.

26. Fernando Ortiz, *Los bailes y el teatro*, pp. 162–75.

27. Lawrence W. Levine makes this point about the liberating qualities of slave religion. He writes, "Slave music, slave religion, slave folk beliefs—the entire sacred world of the black slaves—created the necessary space between the slaves and their owners and were the means of preventing legal slavery from becoming spiritual slavery. In addition to the world of the masters which slaves inhabited and accommodated to, as they had to, they created and maintained a world apart which they shared with each other and which remained their own domain, free of control of those who ruled the earth" (*Black Culture and Black Consciousness: Afro-American Folk Thought from Slavery to Freedom* [New York: Oxford University Press, 1977], p. 80).

11: SYMBIOSIS

1. Karl Marx, "Toward the Critique of Hegel's Philosophy of Law" (1843), in *Writings of the Young Marx*, edited by Lloyd D. Easton and Kurt H. Guddat (Garden City, N.Y.: Doubleday, 1967), p. 250.

2. See Eugene D. Genovese, *Roll, Jordan, Roll: The World the Slaves Made* (New York: Random House, 1972), pp. 161–68; and Raboteau, *Slave Religion*, pp. 290–318.

3. For some examples of this selective interpretation of the Gospel, see Charles Joyner, *Down by the Riverside: A South Carolina Slave Community* (Urbana: University of Illinois Press, 1984), pp. 154–59.

4. See Douglass in Raboteau, *Slave Religion*, pp. 247–48.

5. Moreno, *The Sugarmill*, p. 54.

6. This oath is reproduced in Jean Price-Mars, *So Spoke the Uncle* (Washington, D.C.: Three Continents Press, 1983), pp. 47–48 (original French edition published in 1928). Alfred Metraux tells the story of the role of *vodun* in the Haitian revolution at some length (see *Voodoo in Haiti* [New York: Schocken, 1972], pp. 41–49).

7. See Leonard E. Barrett, *The Rastafarians: Sounds of Cultural Dissonance* (Boston: Beacon, 1977); and Joseph Owens, *Dread: The Rastafarians of Jamaica* (London: Heinemann, 1979).

8. See Gayraud S. Wilmore, *Black Religion and Black Radicalism*, 2d ed. (Maryknoll, N.Y.: Orbis, 1983), pp. 57–73.

9. Montejo, *Autobiography*, p. 26.

10. One of the first people to write about the malign power of African-derived medicine was the indefatiguable researcher Zora Neale Hurston (see *Tell My Horse* [Philadelphia: Lippincott, 1938], pp. 251–57). Ethnobotanist Wade Davis verifies the ingredients of Haitian poisons in *The Serpent and the Rainbow*.

11. Montejo, *Autobiography*, pp. 143–44.

12. For a discussion on the uses of "syncretism" as an explanatory category in the study of religion, see Baird, *Category Formation in the History of Religions*, pp. 142–52.

13. Herskovits, "African Gods and Catholic Saints," pp. 635–36.

14. Metraux, *Voodoo in Haiti*, p. 324.

15. Ibid.

16. I must admit that I have never been able to get much confirmation for this interpretation. When I have asked *santeros* if the chromolithographs represent human beings being mounted by the *orishas*, I have received answers such as, "Oh, yes," or, "I don't know."

17. Bastide, *African Civilisations in the New World*, p. 154.

18. I am indebted to Leslie G. Desmangles for the application of this term to the relationship between African and Christian religions in the New World (see "The Vodun Loas: A Case in Cultural Symbiosis" [Ph.D. diss., Temple University, 1975]).

19. Bastide, *The African Religions of Brazil*, p. 272.

20. I have heard several older *santeros* lament the younger generation's laxity about prayer to the *orishas* in Lucumi. They look on prayer to the *orishas* in Spanish as a kind of sacrilege that the *orishas* will not countenance for long.

21. Bastide, *African Civilisations in the New World*, p. 155.

22. Ibid., p. 156.

23. I am indebted to Sister Mary Ann Borrello of New York, who told me in a personal communication that her work with Puerto Rican spiritualists had led her to model ideas of religious syncretism on bilingualism (see Mary Ann Borrello and Elizabeth Mathias, "Botanicas: Puerto Rican Folk Pharmacies," *Natural History*, vol. 86, no. 7 [August/ September 1977]).

12: THE RELIGION

1. The terms "emic" and "etic" have their origin in the work of Kenneth Pike, who found that the distinction between phonemic and phonetic in structural linguistics could be applied to methods of cultural description (see *Language in Relation to a Unified Theory of the Structure of Human Behavior* [Glendale, Calif.: Summer Institute of Linguistics, 1954], vol. 1). Through the writings of Charles O. Frake, these terms have been taken up and broadened by a number of cultural anthropologists to distinguish native (emic) and nonnative (etic) categories of interpretation (see "The Ethnographic Study of Cognitive Systems," in *Anthropology and Human Behavior*, edited by Thomas Gladwin and William C. Sturtevant [Washington, D.C.: Anthropological Society of Washington, 1962]). At their broadest, these terms are a way of using a linguistic model to distinguish and make use of the different interpretations of reality made by insiders and by outsiders.

2. See *Max Weber on the Methodology of the Social Sciences*, translated and edited by Edward A. Shils and Henry A. Finch (Glencoe, Ill.: Free Press, 1949), esp. pp. 82–112.

3. Joachim Wach, "The Meaning and Task of the History of Religions (*Religionswissenschaft*)," in *The History of Religions: Essays on the Problem of Understanding*, edited by Joseph Kitagawa (Chicago: University of Chicago Press, 1967), p. 13. Wilhelm Dilthey defines the problem of hermeneutics in this way: "Interpretation would be impossible if expressions of life were completely strange. It would be unnecessary if nothing strange were in them. It lies, therefore, between these two extremes. It is always required where something strange is to be grasped through the art of understanding" (*Pattern and Meaning in History: Thoughts on History and Society* [New York: Harper & Row, 1962], p. 77).

4. Rudolf Otto, *The Idea of the Holy* (1917; reprint, Oxford: Oxford University Press, 1958), p. 8.

5. The discipline called history of religions has been concerned with the development of a distinctive method for the study of religion. For a

short history of the discipline, see Mircea Eliade, "The History of Religions in Retrospect: 1912 and After," in *The Quest: History and Meaning in Religion* (Chicago: University of Chicago Press, 1969). On the question of understanding religions, see Gerardus van der Leeuw, *Religion in Essence and Manifestation* (1933; reprint, New York: Harper & Row, 1963), 2: 671–78; Ernst Benz, "On Understanding Non-Christian Religions," in *The History of Religions: Essays in Methodology*, edited by Mircea Eliade and Joseph M. Kitagawa (Chicago: University of Chicago Press, 1959); and Baird, *Category Formation in the History of Religions*, pp. 54–125.

The Norwegian phenomenologist of religion William Brede Kristensen is critical of Otto yet maintains the necessity of an interpretation based on the believer's perspective. He writes, "We gain a different conception of the 'holy' when we take the reality of the believers' faith as our starting point than when we choose to take the 'essence' of religion in general as the starting point. This reality proves to be self-subsistent and absolute; it is beyond all our rational criticism. The only difficulty for us is to form an accurate conception of this reality and to understand it from within" (*The Meaning of Religion* [The Hague: Martinus Nijhoff, 1971], p. 23).

6. Otto, *The Idea of the Holy*, pp. 5–40.

7. Mircea Eliade, *The Sacred and the Profane* (New York: Harcourt, Brace & World, 1959).

8. Ibid., p. 100.

9. Ibid., p. 96.

10. Placide Tempels, *Bantu Philosophy* (1945; reprint, Paris: Presence Africaine, 1959). Tempels has had many critics through the years who have attacked both his motive of religious conversion and his use of Western philosophical ideas such as the *élan vital* of Henri Bergson to frame his contrast between "Bantu" and "Western" ontologies. For an excellent review of these critiques, see Paulin J. Hountondji, *African Philosophy: Myth or Reality* (Bloomington: Indiana University Press, 1983), esp. pp. 33–46. See also the essays in *African Philosophy: An Introduction*, edited by Richard A. Wright, 3d ed. (Lanham, Md.: University Press of America, 1984).

11. It is R. R. Marrett who is responsible for the often-quoted phrase, "savage religion is not so much something thought out as danced out" (*The Threshold of Religion* [London: Methuen, 1909], p. xxi). For a superb discussion of early anthropology's attempts to interpret "prim-

itive" religion, see E. E. Evans-Pritchard, *Theories of Primitive Religion* (Oxford: Clarendon, 1965).

12. See Sheila S. Walker, *Ceremonial Spirit Possession in Africa and Afro-America* (Leiden: Brill, 1972), pp. 147–48.

13. Idowu, *Olodumare*, p. 60. Idowu's etymology of *orisha* as "head source" is disputed by several Yoruba scholars, but none has provided a satisfactory interpretation. For some of the pitfalls of Yoruba etymology, see Modupe Oduyoye, *The Vocabulary of Yoruba Religious Discourse* (Ibadan: Daystar, 1972).

14. The best review of the monotheism/polytheism discussions among scholars of African religions is Booth, "God and the Gods in West Africa." Booth quotes Paul Tillich on the subject as follows: "The concreteness of man's ultimate concern drives him toward polytheistic structures; the reaction of the absolute element against these drives him toward monotheistic structures" (p. 176).

15. An interesting treatment of the principles of divination can be found in Jung's introduction to the ancient Chinese book of divination, the *I Ching*, translated by Cary F. Baynes, 3d ed. (Princeton, N.J.: Princeton University Press, 1967). For a fuller treatment of the cogency of Jung's ideas of divination, see Ira Progoff, *Jung, Synchronicity, and Human Destiny* (New York: Julian, 1973).

16. On the idea of sacrifice as a gift, see Henri Hubert and Marcel Mauss, *Sacrifice: Its Nature and Function* (1899; reprint, Chicago: University of Chicago Press, 1964). The theoretical framework for sacrifice as a ritual of commensalism can be found in William Robertson Smith, *The Religion of the Semites* (1889; reprint, New York: Meridian, 1956). Awolalu finds six categories of Yoruba sacrifice: thanksgiving and communion; votive; propitiatory; preventative; substitutionary; and foundation (*Yoruba Beliefs and Sacrificial Rites*, pp. 143–61). For a provocative examination of sacrifice as social and psychological substitution, see Rene Girard, *Violence and the Sacred* (Baltimore: Johns Hopkins University Press, 1977). A *santera* once told me that she had to offer an animal to an *orisha* because the *orisha* was the cause of her child's illness. She said that the saint wanted the life of the child and that she had to "give to the saint the life it wants."

17. Bascom, "Two Forms of Afro-Cuban Divination," p. 176.

18. Dominique Zahan, *The Religion, Spirituality, and Thought of Traditional Africa* (Chicago: University of Chicago Press, 1979), p. 33.

19. Cabrera, *Yemayá y Ochún*, p. 134.

20. The Haitian physician Louis Mars in his examination of *vodun* possession speaks of "theocentric states" (*The Crisis of Possession in Voodoo* (1946), translated by Kathleen Collins [Berkeley: Reed, Cannon & Johnson, 1977]). There may be several kinds of trance—levels of mystical union between human and divine consciousness—that are recognized by *santeros*. Since every ceremony seems to involve as many people being pulled out of altered states as people guided into them, I am led to think that santería initiates can identify several different states of trance awareness. As an outsider, this mystical psychology has never been made known to me, and I have only observed what seems to me to be "full" and "partial" states of trance.

21. In chap. 8 above, I wrote that I think this "mounting" activity of the *orisha* has a sexual interpretation, though I have only received hints of this from *santeros*. The description of the medium as a wife of the *orisha*, the idea of union in trance, the medium's inability to remember his or her experience while in union with the *orisha*, all suggest a profound sexual experience. The use of sexual symbolism to describe mystical union of human and divine is a worldwide phenomenon and perfectly applicable to santería trance.

22. See Ortiz, *Los bailes y el teatro*, esp. pp. 200–201.

23. Verger, *Notes*, p. 72.

24. Walker, *Ceremonial Spirit Possession*, pp. 167–68.

25. For a review of sociological and psychological theories of trance, see I. M. Lewis, *Ecstatic Religion: An Anthropological Study of Spirit Possession and Shamanism* (Baltimore: Penguin, 1971).

GLOSSARY

Readers seeking more information on these and many, many other santería terms should consult Lydia Cabrera's invaluable *Anago: vocabulario Lucumi* (Miami: Ediciónes Universal, 1970).

Achere (ah-chay-RAY): Musical instrument sacred to Shango, gourd rattle.

Afrocubanisma: Cuban literary and cultural movement of the mid-twentieth century emphasizing native Cuban cultural values.

Alafia: Health, goodness; a sign of *dilogun* divination.

Alafin (ah-la-FEEN): Title of the kings of Oyo.

Aleyo: An uninitiated devotee.

Aña: The fundamental spirit of the drum.

Apalencado: A slave runaway living in a *palenque.*

Ara orun (ah-RAH aw-ROON): "The people of heaven." Yoruba ancestors or *orishas,* depending on context.

Arara (ah-RAH-RAH): Fon communities in Cuba.

Ashe (ah-SHAY): Power, grace, growth, blood. The life force of God, the *orishas,* and nature.

Asientada: An initiate. One who has undergone *asiento.*

Asiento: Central ceremony of initiation into santería in which the *orisha* is "seated" in the head.

Awole: An Alafin of Old Oyo.

Babalawo (bah-bah-LAH-woe): "Father of the mystery." Ifa diviner, priest of Orunmila, and high priest of santería.

Babalocha (bah-bah-LOW-cha): "Father of/in the *orisha*." Priest of a specific *orisha*.

Babaluaye (bah-bah-LOO-eye-ay): Awesome *orisha* of the transformative power of disease.

BaKongo: Influential African ethnic group in Cuba.

Bata (bah-TAH): Sacred double-headed drums.

Batea Shango: Wooden bowl and mortar pedestal for the fundamental symbols of Shango.

Bembe (bem-BAY): Drum and dance festival for the *orishas*.

Bohío: Country "shack" of Cuban folklore.

Botánica: Retail shop specializing in santería paraphernalia, especially "botanicals," that is, herbs.

Cabildo: Any assembly, often a municipal council or cathedral chapter. Specifically an Afro-Cuban social club and cult association.

Camino: Literally "road" or "path." In santería, a manifestation or mythic representation of an *orisha*. Every *orisha* is acknowledged according to several *caminos*.

Canastillero: A shelved cabinet with closing doors acting as an altar for the *orisha* stones.

Caridad del Cobré: Roman Catholic devotion to the Virgin Mary. Our Lady of Charity of the town of Cobré in eastern Cuba. Patron saint of the island.

Cascarilla: Ritual chalk made from dried egg whites (cf. *efun*).

Cimarrón: "Wild man," runaway slaves living in the interior of the island. Maroon.

Coartación: Legal process allowing slaves to purchase their own freedom.

Collar de mazo: Massive beaded necklace of initiates.

Comparsa: Carnival group.

Coronación: Dramatic point in *asiento* initiation when the *orisha* is "crowned," "enthroned," or "seated" in the devotee's head.

Criollo: Creole, New World born, of heterogeneous origin.

Dahomey: African kingdom, neighbors to the Yoruba, of particular influence in the eighteenth and nineteenth centuries.

GLOSSARY

Derecho: Fee taken for ritual work.

Día del medio: "Middle Day" of *asiento* ceremony.

Día de reyes: Day of Kings. Epiphany. A feast celebrated with great processions and dancing by Afro-Cubans in colonial Cuba.

Dilogun (dee-low-GOON): Divination with sixteen cowrie shells.

Ebo (ay-BOW): Sacrifice. Work.

Ebori eleda (ay-BOW-ree el-ay-DAH): Ritual cleansing of the head.

Efun (ay-FOON): *Cascarilla.* Ritual chalk from dried egg whites.

Egba: Western branch of the Yoruba people.

Egun (ay-GOON): A deceased person. Or a small bone used in Ifa divination.

Egungun (ay-GOON-GOON): Masked cult to Yoruba ancestors.

Ekwele (ek-way-LAY): Divining chain of Ifa (cf. *opele*).

Eleda (el-ay-DAH): The "owner of the head." The "guardian angel."

Eleggua (el-ay-GWAH or el-ay-WAH): *Orisha* messenger, trickster, and "opener of the path."

Eleke (ay-LAY-KAY): Beaded necklace (*collar*) sacred to an *orisha.*

En santo: "In saintliness." In the way of the *orishas.*

Enkangue: Kongo charm.

Ese (ay-SAY): Ifa verse.

Esho (ay-SHOW): "Hold." Call during the *bembe* to hold the rhythm and support the dancer.

Eshu (AY-shoo): In Yorubaland, the principle name for the messenger/trickster spirit. In santería, a *camino* of Eleggua.

Ewe (ay-WAY): Leaves. The sacred herbs of santería.

Ewo (ay-WO): Tabu. Specifically the lifetime tabus or behavioral vows observed as a result of the *ita* divination during initiation.

Ex voto: "Out of a promise." An object symbolic of a devotion to or pact with a sacred being.

Fon: African ethnic group identified with the kingdom of Dahomey. Known in Cuba as Arara.

Fulani: A widely dispersed West African people galvanized by Usuman dan Fodio in the early nineteenth century.

Fundamentos: The "fundamental" symbols of an *orisha*—stones, shells, tools—that transmit his or her *ashe*.

Ga: An African ethnic group living in the coastal area of present-day Ghana.

Gente de color: People of color. Free blacks or nonwhites.

Hacer el santo: "To make the saint." To receive the *fundamentos* of an *orisha*. To have an *orisha* seated in one's head.

Hand of Orula: Preliminary initiation into Ifa.

Ibeji (ee-BAY-jee): Twin child spirits.

Ibo (ee-BOW): Divination sequence in *dilogun* and Ifa that specifies the message by answering yes or no questions.

Ibo: African ethnic group living east of the Niger River. Also rendered "Igbo."

Iboru iboya ibochiche (ee-BOW-ROO ee-BOW-YA ee-BOW-CHEE-chay): "May Ifa accept the sacrifice." Ritual greeting to Ifa and to his priest the *babalawo*.

Ibori (ee-BOW-ree): Ceremonial feeding of the "head" (cf. *ebori eleda*).

Ide (ee-DAY): Wristlet dedicated to the *orishas*, specifically to Orula, the diviner *orisha*. Mark of *babalawo*'s patronage.

Ifa (ee-FAH): The most sophisticated oracle of the Yoruba and of santería. The *orisha* of the oracle.

Ile (ee-LAY): House, community, family. The basic unit of the santería worship community.

Ile igbodu (ee-LAY eeg-bow-DOO): In Yorubaland, a sacred grove of an *orisha*. In santería, a room or area of a house set aside for *orisha* ceremonies.

Ile-Ife (ee-LAY ee-FAY): Spiritual capital of Yorubaland, center of creation.

Ingenio: Sugar mill.

Inle or Erinle (IN-lay or ERR-in-lay): *Orisha* of healing.

Ire (ee-RAY): Good fortune. One alternative of the *ibo* process in Ifa divination.

Iruke (ee-ROO-KAY): Fly whisk, emblem of chiefship and royalty, particularly of Obatala.

Ita (ee-TAH): *Dilogun* divination during *asiento* ceremony. Reveals the destiny and responsibilities of the initiate's life *en santo.*

Italero: One who reads *ita.* Any *dilogun* diviner.

Itotele (ee-TOE-tell-AY): Middle drum of the *bata* orchestra.

Iya (ee-YAH): Mother, wife, senior and largest drum of the *bata* orchestra.

Iyalocha (ee-ya-LOW-cha): Wife of the *orisha,* mother in/of the *orisha. Santera,* priestess of santería.

Iyawo (yah-WOE): Bride of the *orisha,* newborn initiate.

Jihad: Struggle. Militancy on behalf of Islam. Holy war.

Kabiesi (ka-bee-AY-see): Royal title, especially of Shango, "majesty," "unsurpassed."

Kariocha (ka-ree-OH-cha): *Asiento.* The central initiation ceremony of santería.

Kawo Kabiesile (ka-WOE ka-bee-ay-SEE-lay): "Welcome home." Ritual greeting to Shango.

Las Casas: Fra Bartolome de las Casas. Dominican friar witness to the cruelties of the Spanish conquest of the Caribbean. Made royal protector of the Indians.

Letra: Letter. Specifically the forms, figures, or signs of *dilogun* and *ifa* divination.

Limpieza: Cleansing, purification. In santería, a spiritual removal of negative influences, usually concerning the head.

Lucumi (loo-koo-MEE): "My friend." A Yoruba greeting in Cuba. Used to refer to a person of Yoruba descent or to describe any feature of Yoruba culture in Cuba. Sometimes santería is called simply "Lucumi."

Madrina: Godmother. Priestess of santería, a *santera.* Used to refer to a devotee's initiator.

Maferefun (mah-fay-ray-FOON): "Thanks be to."

Manzano: Juan Francisco Manzano (1797–1854), Afro-Cuban poet.

Mayombe: Kongo ethnic group in Cuba. Religion derived from the Mayombe, often considered sorcery by *santeros.*

179

GLOSSARY

Mende: A people of West Africa.

Mesa Blanca: Spiritualist tradition of Latin America.

Moforoibale (mo-fo-ro-EE-bah-lay): "I bow before you." Ritual greeting to *orishas* and *iyalorishas*.

Moyuba (moy-oo-BAH): "I salute you." Name for the litany of invocation to Olodumare, ancestors, *orishas*, and godparents.

Muerto: A dead person, a spirit.

Nación: Nation, specifically an African ethnic group in Cuba.

Ñañigo: Member of the Abakuá society. Popularly thought to be bandits or boogeymen.

Ñañiguismo: The practices of ñañigos.

Negro de nación: African-born Cuban identified with a particular African ethnicity.

Nganga: A priest or object consecrated in the Kongo religious traditions of Cuba.

Obatala (aw-bah-tah-LAH): King of the white cloth. *Orisha* of creation, wisdom, and spiritual clarity.

Obi (oh-BEE): Divination system using coconuts. Personified spirit of the system.

Obinu (oh-bee-NOO): Individual section of the coconut used in *obi*.

Ocha (OH-cha): Hispanicization of *orisha*, often used to refer to the religion itself, as in "La Ocha."

Odu (oh-DOO): Individual divination sign, which includes related proverbs, stories, and sacrifices.

Odudua (oh-DOO-DOO-ah): *Orisha* paired with Obatala to symbolize totality. Co-creator and founder of Ile-Ife.

Ogun (aw-GOON): Warrior-blacksmith *orisha*.

Okonkolo (oh-KON-KO-low): Smallest of the three drums of the *bata* orchestra.

Okpon (awk-PONE): Wooden tray used by *babalawos* to mark signs of divination (cf. *opon*).

Olodumare (oh-low-DOO-may-ray): Almighty God.

Olorisha (oh-low-REE-SHAH): Initiate. One who "has" the *orisha*.

Oluku mi (oh-loo-koo MEE): "My friend." Yoruba greeting, which became the name the Yoruba were known by in Cuba, "Lucumi."

Oluwo (oh-LOO-woe): Highest order of *babalawo*.

Omiero (oh-mee-ERR-OH): Liquid herbal mixture that cools *orishas* and persons.

Omo (OH-moe): "Child." Specifically a child of the *orishas*.

Omo-odu (oh-moe oh-DOO): "Children of the *odu*." The secondary signs of Ifa divination derived from the primary sixteen.

Omo-orisha (OH-moe aw-REE-SHAH): "Child of the *orisha*."

Okpele (awk-pay-LAY): Divining chain of Ifa.

Ori (aw-REE): "Head." The soul or destiny of an individual.

Oriate (aw-REE-ah-tay): Songmaster priest of santería.

Orisha (aw-REE-SHAH): Divine being of santería. *Santo*, saint.

Orisha Oko (aw-REE-SHAH OH-ko): *Orisha* of the farm.

Orula (aw-ROO-lah): Orunmila, Ifa, *orisha* of wisdom and divination.

Orunmila (aw-ROON-mee-la): Orula, Ifa, *orisha* of wisdom and divination.

Osanyin (aw-SIGH-in): *Orisha* of forest leaves. Any herbal preparation.

Oshe (oh-SHAY): Double-headed ax sacred to Shango.

Oshosi (oh-SHOW-see): *Orisha* of the hunt and the mysteries of the forest.

Oshun (aw-SHOON): *Orisha* of the river and fresh water.

Osugbo (oh-SUG-bow): Ill luck in *dilogun* and Ifa divination.

Osun (OH-soon): Staff of the herbalist.

Oya (aw-YAH): *Orisha* of storms, ruler of the dead.

Oyo (AW-yo): Powerful Yoruba kingdom at its height in the seventeenth and eighteenth centuries.

Padrino: Godfather. Priest of santería, a *santero*. Used to refer to one's patron and initiator.

Palenque: Fortified settlement of *cimarrónes* in Cuba's interior.

Palo monte: Kongo religious tradition in Cuba.

Pataki: Story of santería conveyed in the *odu* of *dilogun* or Ifa.

Pilón: Regal mortal stool sacred to Shango.

Pinaldo: The "knife." Ceremony conferring on the children of Ogun the power to sacrifice animals.

Regla: Rule, path, order, or cult. Specifically one of the African religions of Cuba.

Regla de ocha: The path of the *orishas*, santería.

Rogación de la cabeza: Ritual cleansing of the head. *Ebori eleda.*

Santería: The way of the saints.

Santero: Initiate of santería.

Santo: Saint, *orisha*, holiness.

Shango (shan-GO):   *Orisha* of thunder, lightning, and force.

Sopera: Soup tureen. Specifically those bowls in which are kept the stones and other *fundamentos* of the *orishas*.

Suyeres (soo-YAIR-ess):   Lucumi prayers.

Tata: Black nanny.

Usuman dan Fodio: Islamic reformer and founder of the Sokoto caliphate.

Yefa (YAY-fa):   Wood dust on which are marked the *odu* of Ifa.

Yemaya (yeh-mah-YAH):   *Orisha* of the seas and maternal love.

Yubona (ya-BONE-ah):   Sponsor of the initiate for *asiento*.

REFERENCES

A. MAJOR WORKS ON YORUBA RELIGION

Abimbola, Wande. "Iwa Pele: The Concept of Good Character in Ifa Literary Corpus." In *Yoruba Oral Traditions: Poetry in Music, Dance and Drama,* edited by Wande Abimbola. Ife: University of Ife Press, 1975.
————. *Ifa: An Exposition of Ifa Literary Corpus.* Ibadan: Oxford University Press, 1976.
————. *Ifa Divination Poetry.* New York: NOK, 1977.
Abiodun, Rowland. "Ifa Art Objects." In *Yoruba Oral Traditions: Poetry in Music, Dance and Drama,* edited by Wande Abimbola. Ife: University of Ife Press, 1975.
Awolalu, J. O. *Yoruba Beliefs and Sacrificial Rites.* London: Longmans, 1979.
Barber, Karin. "How Man Makes God in West Africa: Yoruba Attitudes toward the Orisa." *Africa,* vol. 51, no. 3 (1981).
Bascom, William R. "The Sociological Role of the Yoruba Cult Group." *Memoirs of the American Anthropological Association,* vol. 63 (1944).
————. "Yoruba Concepts of the Soul." In *Men and Cultures,* edited by Anthony F. Wallace. Philadelphia: University of Pennsylvania Press, 1956.
————. *Ifa Divination: Communication between Gods and Men in West Africa.* Bloomington: Indiana University Press, 1969.
————. *Sixteen Cowries: Yoruba Divination from Africa to the New World.* Bloomington: Indiana University Press, 1980.
Beier, Ulli. *Yoruba Poetry.* Cambridge: Cambridge University Press, 1970.
————. *The Return of the Gods.* Cambridge: Cambridge University Press, 1975.
————. *Yoruba Myths.* Cambridge: Cambridge University Press, 1980.
Carroll, Kevin. *Yoruba Religious Carving.* New York: Praeger, 1967.
Courlander, Harold. *Tales of Yoruba Gods and Heroes.* New York: Crown, 1973.

REFERENCES

Drewal, Henry John, and Margaret Thompson Drewal. *Gelede: Art and Female Power among the Yoruba.* Bloomington: Indiana University Press, 1983.

Epega, D. Olarimwa. *The Basis of Yoruba Religion.* Abeokuta: Ijamido Printers, n.d.

Farrow, Stephen S. *Faith, Fancies and Fetish; or, Yoruba Paganism.* London: Society for Promoting Christian Knowledge, 1926.

Gleason, Judith. *Orisha: The Gods of Yorubaland.* New York: Atheneum, 1971.

———. *A Recitation of Ifa, Oracle of the Yoruba.* New York: Grossman, 1973.

Idowu, E. Bolaji. *Olodumare: God in Yoruba Belief.* London: Longmans, 1962.

Lawal, Babatunde. *Yoruba Sango Sculpture in Historical Retrospect.* Ph.D. dissertation, Indiana University, 1970.

———. "The Living Dead: Art and Immortality among the Yoruba of Nigeria." *Africa*, vol. 47, no. 1 (1977).

Lucas, J. Olodumide. *The Religion of the Yorubas.* Lagos: C.M.S. Bookshop, 1948.

McClelland, E. M. *The Cult of Ifa among the Yoruba.* Volume 1. London: Ethnographica, 1982.

Morton-Williams, Peter M. "An Outline of the Cosmology and Cult Organization of the Oyo Yoruba." *Africa*, vol. 34, no. 3 (1964).

Oduyoye, Modupe. *The Vocabulary of Yoruba Religious Discourse.* Ibadan: Daystar, 1971.

Parrinder, Geoffrey. "Theistic Beliefs of the Yoruba and Ewe Peoples of West Africa." In *African Ideas of God,* edited by Edwin W. Smith. London: Edinburgh House, 1950.

———. *Religion in an African City.* London: Oxford University Press, 1953.

Pemberton, John, III. "A Cluster of Sacred Symbols: Orisa Worship among the Igbomina Yoruba of Ila-Orangun." *History of Religions,* vol. 17, no. 1 (August 1977).

Pemberton, John, III, with Fagg, William, and Holcombe, Bryce. *Yoruba Sculpture of West Africa.* New York: Knopf, 1982.

Prince, Raymond. *Ifa: Yoruba Divination and Sacrifice.* Ibadan: Ibadan University Press, 1966.

Simpson, George Eaton. *Yoruba Religion and Medicine in Ibadan.* Ibadan: Ibadan University Press, 1980.

Thompson, Robert Farris. *Black Gods and Kings.* Bloomington: Indiana University Press, 1976.

———. *Flash of the Spirit: African and Afro-American Art and Philosophy.* New York: Random House, 1983.

Verger, Pierre. *Notes sur le culte des orisa et vodun.* Dakar: L'Institut Français d'Afrique Noire, 1957.

———. "The Yoruba High God: A Review of the Sources." *Odu,* n. s., vol. 2, no. 2 (1966).

————. "Trance and Convention in Nago-Yoruba Spirit Mediumship." In *Spirit Mediumship and Society*, edited by John Beattie and John Middleton. New York: Africana, 1969.

————. "Trance States in Orisha Worship." *Odu*, o.s., no. 9 (September 1963).

Wenger, Susanne, and Gert Chesi. *A Life with the Gods: In Their Yoruba Homeland*. Worgl: Perlinger, 1983.

B. MAJOR WORKS ON *SANTERÍA*

Angarica, Nicolas V. *Manual del orihate (religión Lucumi)*. Miami: Ediciones Universal, 1979.

Barreal, Isaac. "Tendencias sincreticas de los cultos populares en Cuba." *Etnologia y folklore*, vol. 1 (1966).

Bascom, William R. "The Focus of Cuban Santería." *Southwestern Journal of Anthropology*, vol. 6, no. 1 (1950).

————. "Two Forms of Afro-Cuban Divination." In *Acculturation in the Americas*, edited by Sol Tax. Chicago: University of Chicago Press, 1952.

————. *Shango in the New World*. Austin: University of Texas, African and Afro-American Research Institute, 1972.

————. *Sixteen Cowries: Yoruba Divination from Africa to the New World*. Bloomington: Indiana University Press, 1980.

Brandon, George Edward. *The Dead Sell Memories: An Anthropological Study of Santeria in New York City*. Ann Arbor: University Microfilms, 1983.

Brown, David Hiliary. *Garden in the Machine: Afro-Cuban Sacred Art and Performance in Urban New Jersey and New York*. Ph.D. dissertation, Yale University, 1989.

Cabrera, Lydia. *Anagó: vocabulario Lucumi*. Miami: Ediciones Universal, 1970.

————. *La laguna sagrada de San Joaquín* (Madrid: Ediciónes R, 1973).

————. *El monte*. Miami: Ediciones Universal, 1975.

————. *Koeko iyawó: aprende novicia*. Miami: Ediciones Universal, 1980.

————. *Yemayá y Ochún*. Miami: Ediciones Universal, 1980.

Canet, Carlos. *Lucumí: religión de los Yorubas en Cuba*. Miami: AIP Publications Center, 1973.

Castellanos, Isabel Mercedes. *The Use of Language in Afro-Cuban Religion*. Ph.D. dissertation, Georgetown University, 1976.

Cornelius, Steven Harry. *The Convergence of Power: An Investigation into the Music Liturgy of Santería in New York City*. Ph.D. dissertation, University of California at Los Angeles, 1989.

Cortés, Enrique. *Manual del oriaté*. New York: Vilaragut Articulos Religiosos, 1980.

Díaz Fabelo, Teodoro. *Olórun*. Havana: Departamento de Folklore del Teatro Nacional de Cuba, 1960.

REFERENCES

Edwards, Gary, and John Mason. *Black Gods: Orisa Studies in the New World.* New York: Yoruba Theological Archministry, 1985.

Efúnde, Agún. *Los secretos de la santería.* Miami: Ediciones Cubamérica, 1978.

Elizondo, Carlos. *Manual del italero de la religion Lucumi.* N.p., n.d.

Fall, Noeye Anna. *La santería dans la société cubaine.* Dakar: Centre de Haute Etudes, 1975.

Fernandez, Vivian Eloise. *The Effects of Spiritism and/or Santería on Psychiatric Diagnosis of Puerto Ricans in New York City.* Ph.D. dissertation, Adelphi University, 1986.

Friedman, Robert Alan. *Making an Abstract World Concrete: Knowledge, Competence and Structural Dimensions of Performance among Bata Drummers in Santeria.* Ph.D. dissertation, Indiana University, 1982.

Garcia Cortez, Julio. *El Santo.* Mexico, D. F.: Editora Latino Americana, 1971.

———. *Pataki: leyendas y misterios de los orishas africanos.* Miami: Ediciones Universal, 1980.

Gleason, Judith. *Santería, Bronx.* New York: Atheneum, 1975.

———. *Oya: In Praise of the Goddess.* Boston: Shambala, 1987.

Gonzáles Huguet, Lydia. "La casa-templo en la regla de ocha." *Etnología y folklore,* vol. 5 (January–June 1968).

González-Wippler, Migene. *Santería: African Magic in Latin America.* Garden City, N.Y.: Doubleday/Anchor, 1973.

———. *The Santería Experience.* Englewood Cliffs, N.J.: Prentice-Hall, 1982.

———. *Rituals and Spells of Santería.* New York: Original Publications, 1984.

———. *Tales of the Orishas.* New York: Original Publications, 1985.

Gregory, Steven. *Santería in New York City: A Study in Cultural Resistance.* Ph.D. dissertation, New School for Social Research, 1986.

Lachatañere, Romulo. *Manual de santería: el sistema de cultos "Lucumis."* Havana: Editorial Caribe, 1942.

López, Lourdes. *Estudio de un babalao.* Havana: Universidad de Havana, Departamento de Actividades Culturales, 1978.

Ortiz, Fernando. *Los bailes y el teatro de los negros en el folklore de Cuba.* Havana: Ediciones Cardenas, 1951.

Perez, Cecilio. *Ita: Mythology of the Yoruba People.* Miami: Obaecun Books, 1989.

Pichardo, Ernesto, and Lourdes Nieto. *Oduduwa Obatala.* Miami: Church of Lukumi Babaluaye, 1984.

Rogers, Andres R. *Los caracoles: historia de sus letras.* Washington, D.C.: Librería Latinoamericana, 1973.

Sánchez, Julio. *La religión de los orichas.* Hato Rey: Colección Estudios Afrocaribeños, 1978.

Sandoval, Mercedes Cros. *La religión afrocubana.* Madrid: Playor, 1975.

INDEX

187